My Doll Organizer©
Fact Sheets Album

Over 60 Fact Sheets

19-inch pair of 143 Kestner children. From the book *Kestner King of Dollmakers*. *Mary Lou Rubright Collection. Photograph by Howard Foulke.*

Hobby House Press, Inc.
Grantsville, MD 21536
www.hobbyhouse.com

© 2000 Hobby House Press, Inc.

My Doll Organizer©

22-inch 192 Kestner, all original. From the book *Kestner King of Dollmakers*. *J.C. Collection. Photograph by Howard Foulke.*

Congratulations! You have just taken the first step towards organizing your doll collection!

One of the most enjoyable aspects of collecting is in the categorizing, researching and keeping track of the market value of the dolls we collect. At first remembering everything about our collection is easy, but the larger the collection gets, or the longer we collect, the more difficult it is to recall all the details of the individual dolls.

Record Keeping is Important

This organizer makes it easy to keep all of the relevant information about your individual dolls at your fingertips. It won't matter if you've had the doll for two weeks, two months, two years or two decades – all of the things you need to know will be kept together.

You may wonder why keeping a record of your collection is important. If ever you decide to insure your collection, information about the value of your dolls is paramount. If you decide someday to sell your collection, or a worse case scenario, if your dolls would be stolen or damaged by a natural disaster or fire, all the information you will need to make decisions will be in one place. If something should happen to you, having complete records of your collection will ensure that your loved ones understand the value of the dolls.

Plastic Pockets for Stuff

Most modern dolls come with information such as wrist tags and certificates of authenticity that you may choose not to display with your doll. What better way to keep them together than to file them in one of the plastic pockets in this binder? For any doll, antique or modern, the pockets are also a place to keep your sales receipt with the information about where, when, and from whom you bought the doll and how much you paid.

Organize your My Doll Organizer© (separate 3-ring notebook Item #5699) so that the plastic pockets will be with the coordinating information pages where you have recorded the description and important details about the dolls. You may wish to keep track of your collection by numbering each doll and matching to the information pages, or you may want to identify them by name or some other way. Just make sure that the doll has some kind of identification (perhaps with a tie-on tag or cloth label inconspicuously attached to the clothing) and that the page and plastic pocket with information about that doll is keyed the same way.

The organizer is the perfect place to keep any brochures, advertisements, or articles you find relating to your dolls. If you ever need to give a program at doll club, or choose to write an article about your dolls, you will have everything you need at your fingertips. Organizing your dolls will also be a way you can avoid duplicating dolls and easily figure out what "holes" are in your collection to be filled. (Okay, why not use this as an excuse to keep collecting!)

Doll Facts

The front of the record form has room for a photograph of the doll and space for both head and body marks. These are very important for identification. If the doll has all original clothing, you will want to make certain that you include the costume in the photo. For some antique dolls where the details of the face are very important, you may want to include a close-up "portait" picture.

With some dolls the marks are critical in identification. Up until the law in 1891 which required that all imports to the USA be marked, many of the antique dolls from Europe were unmarked or carried only marks important to the manufacturer. The doll's heads are almost always marked in some form on the back of the neck with the country of origin and usually some kind of a manufacturer's mark. The bisque dolls often have a mold number (indicating a particular face) and a size number as well. (In those instances the size number would indicate centimeters, not inches.) Ball-jointed composition bodies were probably ink-stamped or had a paper label. These tended to fade, disappear or peel off during play, so many bodies may be unmarked. Later dolls may carry marks on their heads, bodies, even soles of the feet. And most modern dolls carry paper documentation when originally marketed. The value of your dolls will be safeguarded if you have all of the original paperwork intact.

Calin pink and blue striped by Corolle.

The first part of the record form asks for basic information such as the category or type – is the doll an "antique" (roughly over 75 years old), "collectible" (30 to 75 years old), "modern" (less than 30 years old) or an artist's doll? You can break the categories down further, for example, "modern fashion doll," a specific doll brand, or "antique French fashion."

Probably the most important section to fill out is on the front, under the doll's name, maker and height, where you record information about your initial purchase. This is where you will keep track of the doll's replacement value, and probably update it every year or so. There are many sources for infor-

mation about dolls' secondary values. A good reference is Jan Foulke's *Blue Book of Dolls and Values.* Revised versions are published periodically which contain current values for both antique and modern dolls. In addition, there are numerous price guides about specific dolls like Madame Alexander dolls, *Ginny, Barbie*®, and so on. Doll shows, doll magazines, auctions, doll shops and the internet are all other good sources for current doll prices.

Maintaining a record of your dolls' current value is very important for insurance purposes or if you ever decide to put some of your dolls up for "adoption." (Perhaps as a way to finance an upgrade to your collection.) The organizer allows you to categorize your dolls any way you choose. Perhaps you group them by maker, or by the material they're made of (such as bisque or vinyl), perhaps you will decide to group them chronologically. Since every collection is different, every organizer can be suited to what your specific needs are.

On the back of the form you can record all of the distinguishing details of each doll, including a description of the doll's head where you indicate the fine points about facial features, wig, and so on. There is also an area where you can note details about the doll's body – the way it is jointed and other details and its clothing.

As My Collection Grows, My Doll Organizer Grows too!

There is a variety of products available which can be combined to fit your needs. These products are carried by your favorite bookstore or can be obtained directly from Hobby House Press. Should you wish to obtain more copies of *My Doll Organizer* #5699 ($19.95) or *My Doll Organizer Fact Sheets Album* #5719 ($11.95), or additional *My Organzier Plastic "Stuff" Protectors* #5718 ($6), please contact Hobby House Press at 1-800-554-1447, fax (301) 895-5029 or write to Hobby House Press, Inc., 1 Corporate Drive, Grantsville, MD 21536 or you may order online at www.hobby-house.com.

Other Organizers are available for specific collecting areas, they are: *My Teddy Organizer* #5700 ($19.95), *My Teddy Organizer Fact Sheets Album* #5720 ($11.95), *My Collectibles Organizer* #5725 ($19.95), *My Collectibles Organizer Fact Sheets Album* #5722 ($11.95), *My Antiques Organizer* #5726 ($19.95), and *My Antiques Organizer Fact Sheets Album* #5721 ($11.95).

1999 *Gene "Breathless"*. From the book *Gene*. *Photograph courtesy of Carolyn B. Cook.*

All-original *Patricia-Kin*. *Nancy Carlson Collection.* From the book *Patsy Family Encyclopedia, Vol. II.* *Photograph by David Carlson. Photo courtesy of Patricia N. Schoonmaker.*

Madame Alexander, *Snow White* dressed exclusive to the Disney® classic movie. From the book *A. Glenn Mandeville's Alexander Dolls.* *Photograph courtesy of A. Glenn Mandeville.*

My Doll Organizer©

Doll # _94659_

Head Markings:

Body Markings:

Name of Doll _Gene "Incognito"_

Maker of Doll _Ashton Drake_

Height _15-1/2"_

Acquired from _Catalog_

When acquired _1998_

Purchase price $ _79.95_

Replacement cost (book value) $ _____

Value (date & source) $ _____

_____

Category/Type of doll _Modern_

Condition _Excellent_

_____

_____

Repairs _none_

_____

_____

_____

Done by _____

Repair date _____

Repair cost _____

Original box, tags, other _have all_

packaging

Head

Material (check one)
☐ Bisque ☐ Celluloid ☐ China ☐ Cloth
☐ Composition ☐ Hard Plastic ☐ Papier-mâché
☑ Vinyl ☐ Wax ☐ Wood ☐ Other _____

Type (check one)
☐ Socket ☐ Flange ☐ Shoulder head
☐ Head on shoulder plate ☐ Other _____

Hair (check one)
☐ Wig (☐ Mohair ☐ Human Hair ☑ Synthetic
☐ Other_____)
☐ Molded Hair ☐ Painted ☐ Other _____
Hair color __Blonde__

Eyes (check one)
☐ Glass (☐ Set ☐ Sleeping ☐ Flirty
☐ Paperweight ☐ Threaded)
☐ Decal ☐ Intaglio ☐ Metal ☑ Painted
☐ Eyelashes painted ☐ Hair eyelashes
☐ Synthetic lashes

Mouth (check one)
☑ Closed mouth ☐ Open/Closed ☐ Open mouth
☐ Teeth ☐ Tongue
☐ Other _____

Ears (check one)
☐ Pierced in head ☑ Pierced through lobe
☐ Applied ☐ Other _____

Body (check all appropriate)
☑ Jointed at neck ☐ Elbows ☐ Waist ☐ Wrist
☑ Hips ☐ Knees ☐ Ankles
☑ Other __shoulders__

Torso
Material __Vinyl__

Arms (check one)
☐ Ball jointed ☐ Bent limb ☑ Straight wrist
Material __Vinyl__

Legs (check one)
☐ Ball jointed ☐ Bent limb ☑ Straight
Material __Vinyl__

My Doll Organizer©

Mark(s) on Body
Where located _____
Stamped, incised: _____
Signed by ☐ Artist ☐ Manufacturer

Clothing (check one)
☑ Original to doll ☐ Contemporary with doll

Replacement clothing made by _____
_____

Outerwear
Style __Halter style dress__
_____

Fabric __Cotton__
_____

Color __white with red floral pattern__
_____

Trim_____

Underwear
Fabric _____
_____

Trim_____

Accessories __Chiffon scarf,__
__sunglassess, shoes, nylons,__
__purse and earrings__

References
References: (Book magazine article, internet)
Source, author, page# _____
_____
_____
_____

For a similar doll, see:_____
_____
_____
_____

Ribbons & Awards: _____
_____
_____
_____

My Doll Organizer©

Doll # _____

Photo

Head Markings:

Body Markings:

Name of Doll _____

Maker of Doll _____

Height _____

Acquired from _____

When acquired _____

Purchase price $ _____

Replacement cost (book value) $_____

Value (date & source) $_____

_____

Category/Type of doll _____

Condition _____

Repairs _____

_____

_____

Done by _____

Repair date _____

Repair cost _____

Original box, tags, other _____

_____

_____

Tear carefully along the perforation to remove.

© 2000 Hobby House Press, Inc.

Head

Material (check one)
☐ Bisque ☐ Celluloid ☐ China ☐ Cloth
☐ Composition ☐ Hard Plastic ☐ Papier-mâché
☐ Vinyl ☐ Wax ☐ Wood ☐ Other _____

Type (check one)
☐ Socket ☐ Flange ☐ Shoulder head
☐ Head on shoulder plate ☐ Other _____

Hair (check one)
☐ Wig (☐ Mohair ☐ Human Hair ☐ Synthetic
　　☐ Other_____)
☐ Molded Hair ☐ Painted ☐ Other _____
Hair color _____

Eyes (check one)
☐ Glass (☐ Set ☐ Sleeping ☐ Flirty
　　☐ Paperweight ☐ Threaded)
☐ Decal ☐ Intaglio ☐ Metal ☐ Painted
☐ Eyelashes painted ☐ Hair eyelashes
☐ Synthetic lashes

Mouth (check one)
☐ Closed mouth ☐ Open/Closed ☐ Open mouth
☐ Teeth ☐ Tongue
☐ Other _____

Ears (check one)
☐ Pierced in head ☐ Pierced through lobe
☐ Applied ☐ Other _____

Body (check all appropriate)
☐ Jointed at neck ☐ Elbows ☐ Waist ☐ Wrist
☐ Hips ☐ Knees ☐ Ankles
☐ Other _____

Torso
Material _____

Arms (check one)
☐ Ball jointed ☐ Bent limb ☐ Straight wrist
Material _____

Legs (check one)
☐ Ball jointed ☐ Bent limb ☐ Straight
Material _____

Mark(s) on Body
Where located _____
Stamped, incised: _____
Signed by ☐ Artist ☐ Manufacturer

Clothing (check one)
☐ Original to doll ☐ Contemporary with doll

Replacement clothing made by _____
_____

Outerwear
Style_____
_____

Fabric _____
_____

Color _____

Trim_____

Underwear
Fabric _____
_____

Trim_____

Accessories_____
_____
_____

References
References: (Book magazine article, internet)
Source, author, page# _____
_____
_____

For a similar doll, see:_____
_____
_____

Ribbons & Awards: _____
_____
_____
_____

My Doll Organizer©

Doll # _____

Photo

Head Markings:

Body Markings:

Name of Doll _____

Maker of Doll _____

Height _____

Acquired from _____

    When acquired _____

    Purchase price $ _____

    Replacement cost (book value) $_____

    Value (date & source) $_____

                         _____

Category/Type of doll _____

Condition _____

_____

_____

Repairs _____

_____

_____

    Done by _____

    Repair date _____

    Repair cost _____

Original box, tags, other _____

_____

_____

Head

Material (check one)
☐ Bisque ☐ Celluloid ☐ China ☐ Cloth
☐ Composition ☐ Hard Plastic ☐ Papier-mâché
☐ Vinyl ☐ Wax ☐ Wood ☐ Other _____

Type (check one)
☐ Socket ☐ Flange ☐ Shoulder head
☐ Head on shoulder plate ☐ Other _____

Hair (check one)
☐ Wig (☐ Mohair ☐ Human Hair ☐ Synthetic
　　☐ Other_____)
☐ Molded Hair ☐ Painted ☐ Other _____
Hair color _____

Eyes (check one)
☐ Glass (☐ Set ☐ Sleeping ☐ Flirty
　　☐ Paperweight ☐ Threaded)
☐ Decal ☐ Intaglio ☐ Metal ☐ Painted
☐ Eyelashes painted ☐ Hair eyelashes
☐ Synthetic lashes

Mouth (check one)
☐ Closed mouth ☐ Open/Closed ☐ Open mouth
☐ Teeth ☐ Tongue
☐ Other _____

Ears (check one)
☐ Pierced in head ☐ Pierced through lobe
☐ Applied ☐ Other _____

Body (check all appropriate)
☐ Jointed at neck ☐ Elbows ☐ Waist ☐ Wrist
☐ Hips ☐ Knees ☐ Ankles
☐ Other _____

Torso
Material _____

Arms (check one)
☐ Ball jointed ☐ Bent limb ☐ Straight wrist
Material _____

Legs (check one)
☐ Ball jointed ☐ Bent limb ☐ Straight
Material _____

Mark(s) on Body
Where located _____
Stamped, incised: _____
Signed by ☐ Artist ☐ Manufacturer

Clothing (check one)
☐ Original to doll ☐ Contemporary with doll

Replacement clothing made by _____
_____

Outerwear
Style_____
_____
Fabric_____
_____
Color _____
Trim_____

Underwear
Fabric_____
_____
Trim_____

Accessories_____
_____
_____

References
References: (Book magazine article, internet)
Source, author, page# _____
_____
_____
_____

For a similar doll, see:_____
_____
_____

Ribbons & Awards: _____
_____
_____
_____

My Doll Organizer©

Doll # _____

Photo

Head Markings:

Body Markings:

Name of Doll _____

Maker of Doll _____

Height _____

Acquired from _____

When acquired _____

Purchase price $ _____

Replacement cost (book value) $ _____

Value (date & source) $ _____

_____

Category/Type of doll _____

Condition _____

_____

_____

Repairs _____

_____

_____

_____

Done by _____

Repair date _____

Repair cost _____

Original box, tags, other _____

_____

_____

Head

Material (check one)
- ☐ Bisque ☐ Celluloid ☐ China ☐ Cloth
- ☐ Composition ☐ Hard Plastic ☐ Papier-mâché
- ☐ Vinyl ☐ Wax ☐ Wood ☐ Other_____

Type (check one)
- ☐ Socket ☐ Flange ☐ Shoulder head
- ☐ Head on shoulder plate ☐ Other_____

Hair (check one)
- ☐ Wig (☐ Mohair ☐ Human Hair ☐ Synthetic
       ☐ Other_____)
- ☐ Molded Hair ☐ Painted ☐ Other_____
- Hair color_____

Eyes (check one)
- ☐ Glass (☐ Set ☐ Sleeping ☐ Flirty
       ☐ Paperweight ☐ Threaded)
- ☐ Decal ☐ Intaglio ☐ Metal ☐ Painted
- ☐ Eyelashes painted ☐ Hair eyelashes
- ☐ Synthetic lashes

Mouth (check one)
- ☐ Closed mouth ☐ Open/Closed ☐ Open mouth
- ☐ Teeth ☐ Tongue
- ☐ Other_____

Ears (check one)
- ☐ Pierced in head ☐ Pierced through lobe
- ☐ Applied ☐ Other_____

Body (check all appropriate)
- ☐ Jointed at neck ☐ Elbows ☐ Waist ☐ Wrist
- ☐ Hips ☐ Knees ☐ Ankles
- ☐ Other_____

Torso
- Material _____

Arms (check one)
- ☐ Ball jointed ☐ Bent limb ☐ Straight wrist
- Material _____

Legs (check one)
- ☐ Ball jointed ☐ Bent limb ☐ Straight
- Material _____

Mark(s) on Body
- Where located _____
- Stamped, incised: _____
- Signed by ☐ Artist ☐ Manufacturer

Clothing (check one)
- ☐ Original to doll ☐ Contemporary with doll

Replacement clothing made by _____
_____

Outerwear
- Style_____
  _____
- Fabric _____
  _____
- Color _____
- Trim_____

Underwear
- Fabric _____
  _____
- Trim_____

Accessories_____
_____
_____

References
References: (Book magazine article, internet)
- Source, author, page# _____
  _____
  _____

For a similar doll, see:_____
_____
_____
_____

Ribbons & Awards: _____
_____
_____
_____

My Doll Organizer©

Doll # _____

Photo

Head Markings:

Body Markings:

Name of Doll _____

Maker of Doll _____

Height _____

Acquired from _____

    When acquired _____

    Purchase price $_____

    Replacement cost (book value) $_____

    Value (date & source) $_____

    _____

Category/Type of doll _____

Condition _____

Repairs _____

_____

_____

    Done by _____

    Repair date _____

    Repair cost _____

Original box, tags, other _____

_____

_____

Head

Material (check one)
☐ Bisque ☐ Celluloid ☐ China ☐ Cloth
☐ Composition ☐ Hard Plastic ☐ Papier-mâché
☐ Vinyl ☐ Wax ☐ Wood ☐ Other_____

Type (check one)
☐ Socket ☐ Flange ☐ Shoulder head
☐ Head on shoulder plate ☐ Other_____

Hair (check one)
☐ Wig (☐ Mohair ☐ Human Hair ☐ Synthetic
☐ Other_____)
☐ Molded Hair ☐ Painted ☐ Other _____
Hair color _____

Eyes (check one)
☐ Glass (☐ Set ☐ Sleeping ☐ Flirty
☐ Paperweight ☐ Threaded)
☐ Decal ☐ Intaglio ☐ Metal ☐ Painted
☐ Eyelashes painted ☐ Hair eyelashes
☐ Synthetic lashes

Mouth (check one)
☐ Closed mouth ☐ Open/Closed ☐ Open mouth
☐ Teeth ☐ Tongue
☐ Other _____

Ears (check one)
☐ Pierced in head ☐ Pierced through lobe
☐ Applied ☐ Other _____

Body (check all appropriate)
☐ Jointed at neck ☐ Elbows ☐ Waist ☐ Wrist
☐ Hips ☐ Knees ☐ Ankles
☐ Other _____

Torso
Material _____

Arms (check one)
☐ Ball jointed ☐ Bent limb ☐ Straight wrist
Material _____

Legs (check one)
☐ Ball jointed ☐ Bent limb ☐ Straight
Material _____

Mark(s) on Body
Where located _____
Stamped, incised: _____
Signed by ☐ Artist ☐ Manufacturer

Clothing (check one)
☐ Original to doll ☐ Contemporary with doll

Replacement clothing made by _____
_____

Outerwear
Style_____
_____

Fabric _____
_____

Color _____

Trim_____

Underwear
Fabric _____
_____

Trim_____

Accessories_____
_____
_____

References
References: (Book magazine article, internet)
Source, author, page# _____
_____
_____

For a similar doll, see:_____
_____
_____
_____

Ribbons & Awards: _____
_____
_____
_____

My Doll Organizer©

Doll # _____

Photo

Head Markings:

Body Markings:

Name of Doll _____

Maker of Doll _____

Height _____

Acquired from _____

    When acquired _____

    Purchase price $_____

    Replacement cost (book value) $_____

    Value (date & source) $_____

                 _____

Category/Type of doll _____

Condition _____

Repairs _____

_____

_____

_____

    Done by _____

    Repair date _____

    Repair cost _____

Original box, tags, other _____

_____

_____

_____

Head

Material (check one)
- ☐ Bisque ☐ Celluloid ☐ China ☐ Cloth
- ☐ Composition ☐ Hard Plastic ☐ Papier-mâché
- ☐ Vinyl ☐ Wax ☐ Wood ☐ Other _____

Type (check one)
- ☐ Socket ☐ Flange ☐ Shoulder head
- ☐ Head on shoulder plate ☐ Other _____

Hair (check one)
- ☐ Wig (☐ Mohair ☐ Human Hair ☐ Synthetic
      ☐ Other_____)
- ☐ Molded Hair ☐ Painted ☐ Other _____
- Hair color _____

Eyes (check one)
- ☐ Glass (☐ Set ☐ Sleeping ☐ Flirty
      ☐ Paperweight ☐ Threaded)
- ☐ Decal ☐ Intaglio ☐ Metal ☐ Painted
- ☐ Eyelashes painted ☐ Hair eyelashes
- ☐ Synthetic lashes

Mouth (check one)
- ☐ Closed mouth ☐ Open/Closed ☐ Open mouth
- ☐ Teeth ☐ Tongue
- ☐ Other _____

Ears (check one)
- ☐ Pierced in head ☐ Pierced through lobe
- ☐ Applied ☐ Other _____

Body (check all appropriate)
- ☐ Jointed at neck ☐ Elbows ☐ Waist ☐ Wrist
- ☐ Hips ☐ Knees ☐ Ankles
- ☐ Other _____

Torso
- Material _____

Arms (check one)
- ☐ Ball jointed ☐ Bent limb ☐ Straight wrist
- Material _____

Legs (check one)
- ☐ Ball jointed ☐ Bent limb ☐ Straight
- Material _____

Mark(s) on Body
- Where located _____
- Stamped, incised: _____
- Signed by ☐ Artist ☐ Manufacturer

Clothing (check one)
- ☐ Original to doll ☐ Contemporary with doll

Replacement clothing made by _____
_____

Outerwear
- Style _____
  _____
- Fabric _____
  _____
- Color _____
- Trim _____

Underwear
- Fabric _____
  _____
- Trim _____

Accessories _____
_____
_____

References
References: (Book magazine article, internet)
- Source, author, page# _____
  _____
  _____

For a similar doll, see: _____
_____
_____

Ribbons & Awards: _____
_____
_____
_____

My Doll Organizer©

Doll # _____

Photo

Head Markings:

Body Markings:

Name of Doll _____

Maker of Doll _____

Height _____

Acquired from _____

    When acquired _____

    Purchase price $_____

    Replacement cost (book value) $_____

    Value (date & source) $_____

    _____

Category/Type of doll _____

Condition _____

_____

Repairs _____

_____

_____

    Done by _____

    Repair date _____

    Repair cost _____

Original box, tags, other _____

_____

Head

Material (check one)

☐ Bisque ☐ Celluloid ☐ China ☐ Cloth
☐ Composition ☐ Hard Plastic ☐ Papier-mâché
☐ Vinyl ☐ Wax ☐ Wood ☐ Other_____

Type (check one)

☐ Socket ☐ Flange ☐ Shoulder head
☐ Head on shoulder plate ☐ Other_____

Hair (check one)

☐ Wig (☐ Mohair ☐ Human Hair ☐ Synthetic
          ☐ Other_____)
☐ Molded Hair ☐ Painted ☐ Other_____
Hair color _____

Eyes (check one)

☐ Glass (☐ Set ☐ Sleeping ☐ Flirty
          ☐ Paperweight ☐ Threaded)
☐ Decal ☐ Intaglio ☐ Metal ☐ Painted
☐ Eyelashes painted ☐ Hair eyelashes
☐ Synthetic lashes

Mouth (check one)

☐ Closed mouth ☐ Open/Closed ☐ Open mouth
☐ Teeth ☐ Tongue
☐ Other _____

Ears (check one)

☐ Pierced in head ☐ Pierced through lobe
☐ Applied ☐ Other _____

Body (check all appropriate)

☐ Jointed at neck ☐ Elbows ☐ Waist ☐ Wrist
☐ Hips ☐ Knees ☐ Ankles
☐ Other _____

Torso

Material _____

Arms (check one)

☐ Ball jointed ☐ Bent limb ☐ Straight wrist
Material _____

Legs (check one)

☐ Ball jointed ☐ Bent limb ☐ Straight
Material _____

Mark(s) on Body

Where located _____
Stamped, incised: _____
Signed by ☐ Artist ☐ Manufacturer

Clothing (check one)

☐ Original to doll ☐ Contemporary with doll

Replacement clothing made by _____

_____

Outerwear

Style_____

_____

Fabric _____

_____

Color _____

Trim_____

Underwear

Fabric _____

_____

Trim_____

Accessories_____

_____

_____

References

References: (Book magazine article, internet)

Source, author, page# _____

_____

_____

For a similar doll, see:_____

_____

_____

Ribbons & Awards: _____

_____

_____

_____

My Doll Organizer©

Doll # _____

Tear carefully along the perforation to remove.

Photo

Head Markings:

Body Markings:

Name of Doll _____

Maker of Doll _____

Height _____

Acquired from _____

    When acquired _____

    Purchase price $_____

    Replacement cost (book value) $_____

    Value (date & source) $_____

_____

Category/Type of doll _____

Condition _____

_____

_____

Repairs _____

_____

_____

_____

    Done by _____

    Repair date _____

    Repair cost _____

Original box, tags, other _____

_____

_____

Head

Material (check one)
☐ Bisque ☐ Celluloid ☐ China ☐ Cloth
☐ Composition ☐ Hard Plastic ☐ Papier-mâché
☐ Vinyl ☐ Wax ☐ Wood ☐ Other _____

Type (check one)
☐ Socket ☐ Flange ☐ Shoulder head
☐ Head on shoulder plate ☐ Other _____

Hair (check one)
☐ Wig (☐ Mohair ☐ Human Hair ☐ Synthetic
      ☐ Other_____)
☐ Molded Hair ☐ Painted ☐ Other _____
Hair color _____

Eyes (check one)
☐ Glass (☐ Set ☐ Sleeping ☐ Flirty
      ☐ Paperweight ☐ Threaded)
☐ Decal ☐ Intaglio ☐ Metal ☐ Painted
☐ Eyelashes painted ☐ Hair eyelashes
☐ Synthetic lashes

Mouth (check one)
☐ Closed mouth ☐ Open/Closed ☐ Open mouth
☐ Teeth ☐ Tongue
☐ Other _____

Ears (check one)
☐ Pierced in head ☐ Pierced through lobe
☐ Applied ☐ Other _____

Body (check all appropriate)
☐ Jointed at neck ☐ Elbows ☐ Waist ☐ Wrist
☐ Hips ☐ Knees ☐ Ankles
☐ Other _____

Torso
Material _____

Arms (check one)
☐ Ball jointed ☐ Bent limb ☐ Straight wrist
Material _____

Legs (check one)
☐ Ball jointed ☐ Bent limb ☐ Straight
Material _____

Mark(s) on Body
Where located _____
Stamped, incised: _____
Signed by ☐ Artist ☐ Manufacturer

Clothing (check one)
☐ Original to doll ☐ Contemporary with doll

Replacement clothing made by _____
_____

Outerwear
Style _____
_____

Fabric _____
_____

Color _____

Trim _____

Underwear
Fabric _____
_____

Trim _____

Accessories _____
_____

References
References: (Book magazine article, internet)
Source, author, page# _____
_____
_____

For a similar doll, see: _____
_____
_____

Ribbons & Awards: _____
_____
_____
_____

My Doll Organizer©

Doll # _____

Photo

Head Markings:

Body Markings:

Name of Doll _____

Maker of Doll _____

Height _____

Acquired from _____

    When acquired _____

    Purchase price $ _____

    Replacement cost (book value) $_____

    Value (date & source) $_____

    _____

Category/Type of doll _____

Condition _____

_____

_____

_____

Repairs _____

_____

_____

_____

    Done by _____

    Repair date _____

    Repair cost _____

Original box, tags, other _____

_____

_____

Head

Material (check one)
- ☐ Bisque ☐ Celluloid ☐ China ☐ Cloth
- ☐ Composition ☐ Hard Plastic ☐ Papier-mâché
- ☐ Vinyl ☐ Wax ☐ Wood ☐ Other_____

Type (check one)
- ☐ Socket ☐ Flange ☐ Shoulder head
- ☐ Head on shoulder plate ☐ Other_____

Hair (check one)
- ☐ Wig (☐ Mohair ☐ Human Hair ☐ Synthetic
  - ☐ Other_____)
- ☐ Molded Hair ☐ Painted ☐ Other _____
- Hair color _____

Eyes (check one)
- ☐ Glass (☐ Set ☐ Sleeping ☐ Flirty
  - ☐ Paperweight ☐ Threaded)
- ☐ Decal ☐ Intaglio ☐ Metal ☐ Painted
- ☐ Eyelashes painted ☐ Hair eyelashes
- ☐ Synthetic lashes

Mouth (check one)
- ☐ Closed mouth ☐ Open/Closed ☐ Open mouth
- ☐ Teeth ☐ Tongue
- ☐ Other _____

Ears (check one)
- ☐ Pierced in head ☐ Pierced through lobe
- ☐ Applied ☐ Other _____

Body (check all appropriate)
- ☐ Jointed at neck ☐ Elbows ☐ Waist ☐ Wrist
- ☐ Hips ☐ Knees ☐ Ankles
- ☐ Other _____

Torso
- Material _____

Arms (check one)
- ☐ Ball jointed ☐ Bent limb ☐ Straight wrist
- Material _____

Legs (check one)
- ☐ Ball jointed ☐ Bent limb ☐ Straight
- Material _____

Mark(s) on Body
- Where located _____
- Stamped, incised: _____
- Signed by ☐ Artist ☐ Manufacturer

Clothing (check one)
- ☐ Original to doll ☐ Contemporary with doll

Replacement clothing made by_____
_____

Outerwear
- Style_____
- _____
- Fabric _____
- _____
- Color _____
- Trim_____

Underwear
- Fabric _____
- _____
- Trim_____

Accessories_____
_____
_____

References
References: (Book magazine article, internet)
- Source, author, page# _____
- _____
- _____
- _____

For a similar doll, see:_____
_____
_____
_____

Ribbons & Awards: _____
_____
_____
_____
_____

My Doll Organizer©

Doll # _____

Photo

Head Markings:

Body Markings:

Name of Doll _____

Maker of Doll _____

Height _____

Acquired from _____

   When acquired _____

   Purchase price $ _____

   Replacement cost (book value) $ _____

   Value (date & source) $ _____

_____

Category/Type of doll _____

Condition _____

Repairs _____

_____

_____

   Done by _____

   Repair date _____

   Repair cost _____

Original box, tags, other _____

_____

_____

Head

Material (check one)
- ☐ Bisque ☐ Celluloid ☐ China ☐ Cloth
- ☐ Composition ☐ Hard Plastic ☐ Papier-mâché
- ☐ Vinyl ☐ Wax ☐ Wood ☐ Other _____

Type (check one)
- ☐ Socket ☐ Flange ☐ Shoulder head
- ☐ Head on shoulder plate ☐ Other _____

Hair (check one)
- ☐ Wig (☐ Mohair ☐ Human Hair ☐ Synthetic
  - ☐ Other_____)
- ☐ Molded Hair ☐ Painted ☐ Other _____
- Hair color _____

Eyes (check one)
- ☐ Glass (☐ Set ☐ Sleeping ☐ Flirty
  - ☐ Paperweight ☐ Threaded)
- ☐ Decal ☐ Intaglio ☐ Metal ☐ Painted
- ☐ Eyelashes painted ☐ Hair eyelashes
- ☐ Synthetic lashes

Mouth (check one)
- ☐ Closed mouth ☐ Open/Closed ☐ Open mouth
- ☐ Teeth ☐ Tongue
- ☐ Other _____

Ears (check one)
- ☐ Pierced in head ☐ Pierced through lobe
- ☐ Applied ☐ Other _____

Body (check all appropriate)
- ☐ Jointed at neck ☐ Elbows ☐ Waist ☐ Wrist
- ☐ Hips ☐ Knees ☐ Ankles
- ☐ Other _____

Torso
- Material _____

Arms (check one)
- ☐ Ball jointed ☐ Bent limb ☐ Straight wrist
- Material _____

Legs (check one)
- ☐ Ball jointed ☐ Bent limb ☐ Straight
- Material _____

Mark(s) on Body
- Where located _____
- Stamped, incised: _____
- Signed by ☐ Artist ☐ Manufacturer

Clothing (check one)
- ☐ Original to doll ☐ Contemporary with doll

Replacement clothing made by _____
_____

Outerwear
- Style _____
- _____
- Fabric _____
- _____
- Color _____
- Trim _____

Underwear
- Fabric _____
- _____
- Trim _____

Accessories _____
_____

References
References: (Book magazine article, internet)
- Source, author, page# _____
- _____
- _____

For a similar doll, see: _____
_____
_____

Ribbons & Awards: _____
_____
_____
_____

My Doll Organizer©

Doll # _____

Photo

Head Markings:

Body Markings:

Name of Doll _____

Maker of Doll _____

Height _____

Acquired from _____

    When acquired _____

    Purchase price $_____

    Replacement cost (book value) $_____

    Value (date & source) $_____

    _____

Category/Type of doll _____

Condition _____

_____

_____

Repairs _____

_____

_____

    Done by _____

    Repair date _____

    Repair cost _____

Original box, tags, other _____

_____

_____

Head

Material (check one)
- ☐ Bisque ☐ Celluloid ☐ China ☐ Cloth
- ☐ Composition ☐ Hard Plastic ☐ Papier-mâché
- ☐ Vinyl ☐ Wax ☐ Wood ☐ Other _____

Type (check one)
- ☐ Socket ☐ Flange ☐ Shoulder head
- ☐ Head on shoulder plate ☐ Other _____

Hair (check one)
- ☐ Wig (☐ Mohair ☐ Human Hair ☐ Synthetic
   ☐ Other_____)
- ☐ Molded Hair ☐ Painted ☐ Other _____
- Hair color _____

Eyes (check one)
- ☐ Glass (☐ Set ☐ Sleeping ☐ Flirty
   ☐ Paperweight ☐ Threaded)
- ☐ Decal ☐ Intaglio ☐ Metal ☐ Painted
- ☐ Eyelashes painted ☐ Hair eyelashes
- ☐ Synthetic lashes

Mouth (check one)
- ☐ Closed mouth ☐ Open/Closed ☐ Open mouth
- ☐ Teeth ☐ Tongue
- ☐ Other _____

Ears (check one)
- ☐ Pierced in head ☐ Pierced through lobe
- ☐ Applied ☐ Other _____

Body (check all appropriate)
- ☐ Jointed at neck ☐ Elbows ☐ Waist ☐ Wrist
- ☐ Hips ☐ Knees ☐ Ankles
- ☐ Other _____

Torso
- Material _____

Arms (check one)
- ☐ Ball jointed ☐ Bent limb ☐ Straight wrist
- Material _____

Legs (check one)
- ☐ Ball jointed ☐ Bent limb ☐ Straight
- Material _____

Mark(s) on Body
- Where located _____
- Stamped, incised: _____
- Signed by ☐ Artist ☐ Manufacturer

Clothing (check one)
- ☐ Original to doll ☐ Contemporary with doll

Replacement clothing made by _____
_____

Outerwear
- Style_____
- _____
- Fabric _____
- _____
- Color _____
- Trim_____

Underwear
- Fabric _____
- _____
- Trim_____

Accessories_____
_____
_____

References
References: (Book magazine article, internet)
- Source, author, page# _____
- _____
- _____

For a similar doll, see:_____
_____
_____
_____

Ribbons & Awards: _____
_____
_____
_____

My Doll Organizer©

Doll # _____

Photo

Head Markings:

Body Markings:

Name of Doll _____

Maker of Doll _____

Height _____

Acquired from _____

    When acquired _____

    Purchase price $_____

    Replacement cost (book value) $_____

    Value (date & source) $_____

                 _____

Category/Type of doll _____

Condition _____

_____

_____

Repairs _____

_____

_____

    Done by _____

    Repair date _____

    Repair cost _____

Original box, tags, other _____

_____

_____

Head

Material (check one)
- ☐ Bisque ☐ Celluloid ☐ China ☐ Cloth
- ☐ Composition ☐ Hard Plastic ☐ Papier-mâché
- ☐ Vinyl ☐ Wax ☐ Wood ☐ Other _____

Type (check one)
- ☐ Socket ☐ Flange ☐ Shoulder head
- ☐ Head on shoulder plate ☐ Other _____

Hair (check one)
- ☐ Wig (☐ Mohair ☐ Human Hair ☐ Synthetic
      ☐ Other _____)
- ☐ Molded Hair ☐ Painted ☐ Other _____
- Hair color _____

Eyes (check one)
- ☐ Glass (☐ Set ☐ Sleeping ☐ Flirty
      ☐ Paperweight ☐ Threaded)
- ☐ Decal ☐ Intaglio ☐ Metal ☐ Painted
- ☐ Eyelashes painted ☐ Hair eyelashes
- ☐ Synthetic lashes

Mouth (check one)
- ☐ Closed mouth ☐ Open/Closed ☐ Open mouth
- ☐ Teeth ☐ Tongue
- ☐ Other _____

Ears (check one)
- ☐ Pierced in head ☐ Pierced through lobe
- ☐ Applied ☐ Other _____

Body (check all appropriate)
- ☐ Jointed at neck ☐ Elbows ☐ Waist ☐ Wrist
- ☐ Hips ☐ Knees ☐ Ankles
- ☐ Other _____

Torso
- Material _____

Arms (check one)
- ☐ Ball jointed ☐ Bent limb ☐ Straight wrist
- Material _____

Legs (check one)
- ☐ Ball jointed ☐ Bent limb ☐ Straight
- Material _____

Mark(s) on Body
- Where located _____
- Stamped, incised: _____
- Signed by ☐ Artist ☐ Manufacturer

Clothing (check one)
- ☐ Original to doll ☐ Contemporary with doll

Replacement clothing made by _____
_____

Outerwear
- Style _____
  _____
- Fabric _____
  _____
- Color _____
- Trim _____

Underwear
- Fabric _____
  _____
- Trim _____

Accessories _____
_____
_____

References
References: (Book magazine article, internet)
- Source, author, page# _____
  _____
  _____

For a similar doll, see: _____
_____
_____

Ribbons & Awards: _____
_____
_____
_____

My Doll Organizer©

Doll # _____

Photo

Head Markings:

Body Markings:

Name of Doll _____

Maker of Doll _____

Height _____

Acquired from _____

When acquired _____

Purchase price $ _____

Replacement cost (book value) $_____

Value (date & source) $_____

_____

Category/Type of doll _____

Condition _____

_____

_____

Repairs _____

_____

_____

Done by _____

Repair date _____

Repair cost _____

Original box, tags, other _____

_____

_____

Head

Material (check one)
- ☐ Bisque ☐ Celluloid ☐ China ☐ Cloth
- ☐ Composition ☐ Hard Plastic ☐ Papier-mâché
- ☐ Vinyl ☐ Wax ☐ Wood ☐ Other _____

Type (check one)
- ☐ Socket ☐ Flange ☐ Shoulder head
- ☐ Head on shoulder plate ☐ Other _____

Hair (check one)
- ☐ Wig (☐ Mohair ☐ Human Hair ☐ Synthetic
    ☐ Other_____)
- ☐ Molded Hair ☐ Painted ☐ Other _____
- Hair color _____

Eyes (check one)
- ☐ Glass (☐ Set ☐ Sleeping ☐ Flirty
    ☐ Paperweight ☐ Threaded)
- ☐ Decal ☐ Intaglio ☐ Metal ☐ Painted
- ☐ Eyelashes painted ☐ Hair eyelashes
- ☐ Synthetic lashes

Mouth (check one)
- ☐ Closed mouth ☐ Open/Closed ☐ Open mouth
- ☐ Teeth ☐ Tongue
- ☐ Other _____

Ears (check one)
- ☐ Pierced in head ☐ Pierced through lobe
- ☐ Applied ☐ Other _____

Body (check all appropriate)
- ☐ Jointed at neck ☐ Elbows ☐ Waist ☐ Wrist
- ☐ Hips ☐ Knees ☐ Ankles
- ☐ Other _____

Torso
- Material _____

Arms (check one)
- ☐ Ball jointed ☐ Bent limb ☐ Straight wrist
- Material _____

Legs (check one)
- ☐ Ball jointed ☐ Bent limb ☐ Straight
- Material _____

Mark(s) on Body
- Where located _____
- Stamped, incised: _____
- Signed by ☐ Artist ☐ Manufacturer

Clothing (check one)
- ☐ Original to doll ☐ Contemporary with doll

Replacement clothing made by _____
_____

Outerwear
- Style_____
_____
- Fabric _____
_____
- Color _____
- Trim_____

Underwear
- Fabric _____
_____
- Trim_____

Accessories_____
_____
_____

References
References: (Book magazine article, internet)
- Source, author, page# _____
_____
_____

For a similar doll, see:_____
_____
_____

Ribbons & Awards: _____
_____
_____
_____

My Doll Organizer©

Doll # _____

Photo

Head Markings:

Body Markings:

Name of Doll _____

Maker of Doll _____

Height _____

Acquired from _____

    When acquired _____

    Purchase price $ _____

    Replacement cost (book value) $ _____

    Value (date & source) $ _____

    _____

Category/Type of doll _____

Condition _____

_____

_____

Repairs _____

_____

_____

    Done by _____

    Repair date _____

    Repair cost _____

Original box, tags, other _____

_____

_____

Head

Material (check one)

☐ Bisque ☐ Celluloid ☐ China ☐ Cloth
☐ Composition ☐ Hard Plastic ☐ Papier-mâché
☐ Vinyl ☐ Wax ☐ Wood ☐ Other _____

Type (check one)

☐ Socket ☐ Flange ☐ Shoulder head
☐ Head on shoulder plate ☐ Other _____

Hair (check one)

☐ Wig (☐ Mohair ☐ Human Hair ☐ Synthetic
        ☐ Other_____)
☐ Molded Hair ☐ Painted ☐ Other _____
Hair color _____

Eyes (check one)

☐ Glass (☐ Set ☐ Sleeping ☐ Flirty
        ☐ Paperweight ☐ Threaded)
☐ Decal ☐ Intaglio ☐ Metal ☐ Painted
☐ Eyelashes painted ☐ Hair eyelashes
☐ Synthetic lashes

Mouth (check one)

☐ Closed mouth ☐ Open/Closed ☐ Open mouth
☐ Teeth ☐ Tongue
☐ Other _____

Ears (check one)

☐ Pierced in head ☐ Pierced through lobe
☐ Applied ☐ Other _____

Body (check all appropriate)

☐ Jointed at neck ☐ Elbows ☐ Waist ☐ Wrist
☐ Hips ☐ Knees ☐ Ankles
☐ Other _____

Torso

Material _____

Arms (check one)

☐ Ball jointed ☐ Bent limb ☐ Straight wrist
Material _____

Legs (check one)

☐ Ball jointed ☐ Bent limb ☐ Straight
Material _____

Mark(s) on Body

Where located _____
Stamped, incised: _____
Signed by   ☐ Artist ☐ Manufacturer

Clothing (check one)

☐ Original to doll ☐ Contemporary with doll

Replacement clothing made by _____
_____

Outerwear

Style_____
_____

Fabric _____
_____

Color _____

Trim_____

Underwear

Fabric _____
_____

Trim_____

Accessories_____
_____
_____

References

References: (Book magazine article, internet)
Source, author, page# _____
_____
_____

For a similar doll, see:_____
_____
_____

Ribbons & Awards: _____
_____
_____
_____

My Doll Organizer©

Doll # _____

Photo

Head Markings:

Body Markings:

Name of Doll _____

Maker of Doll _____

Height _____

Acquired from _____

   When acquired _____

   Purchase price $_____

   Replacement cost (book value) $_____

   Value (date & source) $_____

   _____

Category/Type of doll _____

Condition _____

_____

_____

Repairs _____

_____

_____

   Done by _____

   Repair date _____

   Repair cost _____

Original box, tags, other _____

_____

_____

_____

Head

Material (check one)
☐ Bisque ☐ Celluloid ☐ China ☐ Cloth
☐ Composition ☐ Hard Plastic ☐ Papier-mâché
☐ Vinyl ☐ Wax ☐ Wood ☐ Other _____

Type (check one)
☐ Socket ☐ Flange ☐ Shoulder head
☐ Head on shoulder plate ☐ Other _____

Hair (check one)
☐ Wig (☐ Mohair ☐ Human Hair ☐ Synthetic
    ☐ Other_____)
☐ Molded Hair ☐ Painted ☐ Other _____
Hair color _____

Eyes (check one)
☐ Glass (☐ Set ☐ Sleeping ☐ Flirty
    ☐ Paperweight ☐ Threaded)
☐ Decal ☐ Intaglio ☐ Metal ☐ Painted
☐ Eyelashes painted ☐ Hair eyelashes
☐ Synthetic lashes

Mouth (check one)
☐ Closed mouth ☐ Open/Closed ☐ Open mouth
☐ Teeth ☐ Tongue
☐ Other _____

Ears (check one)
☐ Pierced in head ☐ Pierced through lobe
☐ Applied ☐ Other _____

Body (check all appropriate)
☐ Jointed at neck ☐ Elbows ☐ Waist ☐ Wrist
☐ Hips ☐ Knees ☐ Ankles
☐ Other _____

Torso
Material _____

Arms (check one)
☐ Ball jointed ☐ Bent limb ☐ Straight wrist
Material _____

Legs (check one)
☐ Ball jointed ☐ Bent limb ☐ Straight
Material _____

Mark(s) on Body
Where located _____
Stamped, incised: _____
Signed by ☐ Artist ☐ Manufacturer

Clothing (check one)
☐ Original to doll ☐ Contemporary with doll

Replacement clothing made by _____
_____

Outerwear
Style _____
_____

Fabric _____
_____

Color _____

Trim _____

Underwear
Fabric _____
_____

Trim _____

Accessories _____
_____
_____

References
References: (Book magazine article, internet)
Source, author, page# _____
_____
_____

For a similar doll, see: _____
_____
_____

Ribbons & Awards: _____
_____
_____
_____

My Doll Organizer©

Doll # _____

Photo

Head Markings:

Body Markings:

Name of Doll _____

Maker of Doll _____

Height _____

Acquired from _____

    When acquired _____

    Purchase price $_____

    Replacement cost (book value) $_____

    Value (date & source) $_____

    _____

Category/Type of doll _____

Condition _____

Repairs _____

_____

_____

    Done by _____

    Repair date _____

    Repair cost _____

Original box, tags, other _____

_____

_____

Head

Material (check one)

☐ Bisque ☐ Celluloid ☐ China ☐ Cloth
☐ Composition ☐ Hard Plastic ☐ Papier-mâché
☐ Vinyl ☐ Wax ☐ Wood ☐ Other _____

Type (check one)

☐ Socket ☐ Flange ☐ Shoulder head
☐ Head on shoulder plate ☐ Other _____

Hair (check one)

☐ Wig (☐ Mohair ☐ Human Hair ☐ Synthetic
    ☐ Other_____)
☐ Molded Hair ☐ Painted ☐ Other _____
Hair color _____

Eyes (check one)

☐ Glass (☐ Set ☐ Sleeping ☐ Flirty
    ☐ Paperweight ☐ Threaded)
☐ Decal ☐ Intaglio ☐ Metal ☐ Painted
☐ Eyelashes painted ☐ Hair eyelashes
☐ Synthetic lashes

Mouth (check one)

☐ Closed mouth ☐ Open/Closed ☐ Open mouth
☐ Teeth ☐ Tongue
☐ Other _____

Ears (check one)

☐ Pierced in head ☐ Pierced through lobe
☐ Applied ☐ Other _____

Body (check all appropriate)

☐ Jointed at neck ☐ Elbows ☐ Waist ☐ Wrist
☐ Hips ☐ Knees ☐ Ankles
☐ Other _____

Torso

Material _____

Arms (check one)

☐ Ball jointed ☐ Bent limb ☐ Straight wrist
Material _____

Legs (check one)

☐ Ball jointed ☐ Bent limb ☐ Straight
Material _____

Mark(s) on Body

Where located _____
Stamped, incised: _____
Signed by ☐ Artist ☐ Manufacturer

Clothing (check one)

☐ Original to doll ☐ Contemporary with doll

Replacement clothing made by _____
_____

Outerwear

Style_____

Fabric _____
_____

Color _____

Trim_____

Underwear

Fabric _____
_____

Trim_____

Accessories_____
_____
_____

References

References: (Book magazine article, internet)
    Source, author, page# _____
_____
_____

For a similar doll, see:_____
_____
_____

Ribbons & Awards: _____
_____
_____
_____

My Doll Organizer©

Doll # _____

Photo

Head Markings:

Body Markings:

Name of Doll _____

Maker of Doll _____

Height _____

Acquired from _____

    When acquired _____

    Purchase price $ _____

    Replacement cost (book value) $ _____

    Value (date & source) $ _____

    _____

Category/Type of doll _____

Condition _____

_____

_____

Repairs _____

_____

_____

_____

    Done by _____

    Repair date _____

    Repair cost _____

Original box, tags, other _____

_____

_____

Head

Material (check one)

☐ Bisque ☐ Celluloid ☐ China ☐ Cloth
☐ Composition ☐ Hard Plastic ☐ Papier-mâché
☐ Vinyl ☐ Wax ☐ Wood ☐ Other_____

Type (check one)

☐ Socket ☐ Flange ☐ Shoulder head
☐ Head on shoulder plate ☐ Other_____

Hair (check one)

☐ Wig (☐ Mohair ☐ Human Hair ☐ Synthetic
      ☐ Other_____)
☐ Molded Hair ☐ Painted ☐ Other_____
Hair color _____

Eyes (check one)

☐ Glass (☐ Set ☐ Sleeping ☐ Flirty
      ☐ Paperweight ☐ Threaded)
☐ Decal ☐ Intaglio ☐ Metal ☐ Painted
☐ Eyelashes painted ☐ Hair eyelashes
☐ Synthetic lashes

Mouth (check one)

☐ Closed mouth ☐ Open/Closed ☐ Open mouth
☐ Teeth ☐ Tongue
☐ Other _____

Ears (check one)

☐ Pierced in head ☐ Pierced through lobe
☐ Applied ☐ Other _____

Body (check all appropriate)

☐ Jointed at neck ☐ Elbows ☐ Waist ☐ Wrist
☐ Hips ☐ Knees ☐ Ankles
☐ Other _____

Torso

Material _____

Arms (check one)

☐ Ball jointed ☐ Bent limb ☐ Straight wrist
Material _____

Legs (check one)

☐ Ball jointed ☐ Bent limb ☐ Straight
Material _____

Mark(s) on Body

Where located _____
Stamped, incised: _____
Signed by   ☐ Artist ☐ Manufacturer

Clothing (check one)

☐ Original to doll ☐ Contemporary with doll

Replacement clothing made by _____
_____

Outerwear

Style _____
_____

Fabric _____
_____

Color _____

Trim _____

Underwear

Fabric _____
_____

Trim _____

Accessories_____
_____
_____

References

References: (Book magazine article, internet)
Source, author, page# _____
_____
_____

For a similar doll, see: _____
_____
_____

Ribbons & Awards: _____
_____
_____
_____

My Doll Organizer©

Doll # _____

Photo

Head Markings:

Body Markings:

Name of Doll _____

Maker of Doll _____

Height _____

Acquired from _____

   When acquired _____

   Purchase price $ _____

   Replacement cost (book value) $ _____

   Value (date & source) $ _____

      _____

Category/Type of doll _____

Condition _____

_____

_____

Repairs _____

_____

_____

_____

   Done by _____

   Repair date _____

   Repair cost _____

Original box, tags, other _____

_____

_____

Head

Material (check one)
- ☐ Bisque ☐ Celluloid ☐ China ☐ Cloth
- ☐ Composition ☐ Hard Plastic ☐ Papier-mâché
- ☐ Vinyl ☐ Wax ☐ Wood ☐ Other _____

Type (check one)
- ☐ Socket ☐ Flange ☐ Shoulder head
- ☐ Head on shoulder plate ☐ Other _____

Hair (check one)
- ☐ Wig (☐ Mohair ☐ Human Hair ☐ Synthetic
  - ☐ Other _____)
- ☐ Molded Hair ☐ Painted ☐ Other _____
- Hair color _____

Eyes (check one)
- ☐ Glass (☐ Set ☐ Sleeping ☐ Flirty
  - ☐ Paperweight ☐ Threaded)
- ☐ Decal ☐ Intaglio ☐ Metal ☐ Painted
- ☐ Eyelashes painted ☐ Hair eyelashes
- ☐ Synthetic lashes

Mouth (check one)
- ☐ Closed mouth ☐ Open/Closed ☐ Open mouth
- ☐ Teeth ☐ Tongue
- ☐ Other _____

Ears (check one)
- ☐ Pierced in head ☐ Pierced through lobe
- ☐ Applied ☐ Other _____

Body (check all appropriate)
- ☐ Jointed at neck ☐ Elbows ☐ Waist ☐ Wrist
- ☐ Hips ☐ Knees ☐ Ankles
- ☐ Other _____

Torso
- Material _____

Arms (check one)
- ☐ Ball jointed ☐ Bent limb ☐ Straight wrist
- Material _____

Legs (check one)
- ☐ Ball jointed ☐ Bent limb ☐ Straight
- Material _____

Mark(s) on Body
- Where located _____
- Stamped, incised: _____
- Signed by ☐ Artist ☐ Manufacturer

Clothing (check one)
- ☐ Original to doll ☐ Contemporary with doll

Replacement clothing made by _____
_____

Outerwear
- Style _____
  _____
- Fabric _____
  _____
- Color _____
- Trim _____

Underwear
- Fabric _____
  _____
- Trim _____

Accessories _____
_____
_____

References
References: (Book magazine article, internet)
- Source, author, page# _____
  _____
  _____

For a similar doll, see: _____
_____
_____

Ribbons & Awards: _____
_____
_____
_____

My Doll Organizer©

Doll # _____

Photo

Head Markings:

Body Markings:

Name of Doll _____

Maker of Doll _____

Height _____

Acquired from _____

    When acquired _____

    Purchase price $ _____

    Replacement cost (book value) $ _____

    Value (date & source) $ _____

    _____

Category/Type of doll _____

Condition _____

_____

_____

Repairs _____

_____

_____

_____

    Done by _____

    Repair date _____

    Repair cost _____

Original box, tags, other _____

_____

_____

Head

Material (check one)
- ☐ Bisque ☐ Celluloid ☐ China ☐ Cloth
- ☐ Composition ☐ Hard Plastic ☐ Papier-mâché
- ☐ Vinyl ☐ Wax ☐ Wood ☐ Other _____

Type (check one)
- ☐ Socket ☐ Flange ☐ Shoulder head
- ☐ Head on shoulder plate ☐ Other _____

Hair (check one)
- ☐ Wig (☐ Mohair ☐ Human Hair ☐ Synthetic
  - ☐ Other_____)
- ☐ Molded Hair ☐ Painted ☐ Other _____
- Hair color _____

Eyes (check one)
- ☐ Glass (☐ Set ☐ Sleeping ☐ Flirty
  - ☐ Paperweight ☐ Threaded)
- ☐ Decal ☐ Intaglio ☐ Metal ☐ Painted
- ☐ Eyelashes painted ☐ Hair eyelashes
- ☐ Synthetic lashes

Mouth (check one)
- ☐ Closed mouth ☐ Open/Closed ☐ Open mouth
- ☐ Teeth ☐ Tongue
- ☐ Other _____

Ears (check one)
- ☐ Pierced in head ☐ Pierced through lobe
- ☐ Applied ☐ Other _____

Body (check all appropriate)
- ☐ Jointed at neck ☐ Elbows ☐ Waist ☐ Wrist
- ☐ Hips ☐ Knees ☐ Ankles
- ☐ Other _____

Torso
- Material _____

Arms (check one)
- ☐ Ball jointed ☐ Bent limb ☐ Straight wrist
- Material _____

Legs (check one)
- ☐ Ball jointed ☐ Bent limb ☐ Straight
- Material _____

Mark(s) on Body
- Where located _____
- Stamped, incised: _____
- Signed by ☐ Artist ☐ Manufacturer

Clothing (check one)
- ☐ Original to doll ☐ Contemporary with doll

Replacement clothing made by _____
_____

Outerwear
- Style _____
  _____
- Fabric _____
  _____
- Color _____
- Trim _____

Underwear
- Fabric _____
  _____
- Trim _____

Accessories _____
_____
_____

References
References: (Book magazine article, internet)
- Source, author, page# _____
  _____
  _____

For a similar doll, see: _____
_____
_____

Ribbons & Awards: _____
_____
_____
_____

My Doll Organizer©

Doll # _____

Photo

Head Markings:

Body Markings:

Name of Doll _____

Maker of Doll _____

Height _____

Acquired from _____

    When acquired _____

    Purchase price $_____

    Replacement cost (book value) $_____

    Value (date & source) $_____

    _____

Category/Type of doll _____

Condition _____

Repairs _____

_____

_____

_____

    Done by _____

    Repair date _____

    Repair cost _____

Original box, tags, other _____

_____

_____

Head

Material (check one)
☐ Bisque ☐ Celluloid ☐ China ☐ Cloth
☐ Composition ☐ Hard Plastic ☐ Papier-mâché
☐ Vinyl ☐ Wax ☐ Wood ☐ Other_____

Type (check one)
☐ Socket ☐ Flange ☐ Shoulder head
☐ Head on shoulder plate ☐ Other_____

Hair (check one)
☐ Wig (☐ Mohair ☐ Human Hair ☐ Synthetic
          ☐ Other_____)
☐ Molded Hair ☐ Painted ☐ Other_____
Hair color _____

Eyes (check one)
☐ Glass (☐ Set ☐ Sleeping ☐ Flirty
          ☐ Paperweight ☐ Threaded)
☐ Decal ☐ Intaglio ☐ Metal ☐ Painted
☐ Eyelashes painted ☐ Hair eyelashes
☐ Synthetic lashes

Mouth (check one)
☐ Closed mouth ☐ Open/Closed ☐ Open mouth
☐ Teeth ☐ Tongue
☐ Other _____

Ears (check one)
☐ Pierced in head ☐ Pierced through lobe
☐ Applied ☐ Other _____

Body (check all appropriate)
☐ Jointed at neck ☐ Elbows ☐ Waist ☐ Wrist
☐ Hips ☐ Knees ☐ Ankles
☐ Other _____

Torso
Material _____

Arms (check one)
☐ Ball jointed ☐ Bent limb ☐ Straight wrist
Material _____

Legs (check one)
☐ Ball jointed ☐ Bent limb ☐ Straight
Material _____

Mark(s) on Body
Where located _____
Stamped, incised: _____
Signed by ☐ Artist ☐ Manufacturer

Clothing (check one)
☐ Original to doll ☐ Contemporary with doll

Replacement clothing made by _____
_____

Outerwear
Style_____
_____

Fabric _____
_____

Color _____

Trim_____

Underwear
Fabric _____
_____

Trim_____

Accessories_____
_____

References
References: (Book magazine article, internet)
Source, author, page# _____
_____
_____

For a similar doll, see:_____
_____
_____

Ribbons & Awards: _____
_____
_____
_____

My Doll Organizer©

Doll # _____

Photo

Head Markings:

Body Markings:

Name of Doll _____

Maker of Doll _____

Height _____

Acquired from _____

    When acquired _____

    Purchase price $ _____

    Replacement cost (book value) $ _____

    Value (date & source) $ _____

    _____

Category/Type of doll _____

Condition _____

_____

Repairs _____

_____

_____

    Done by _____

    Repair date _____

    Repair cost _____

Original box, tags, other _____

_____

© 2000 Hobby House Press, Inc.

Head

Material (check one)

☐ Bisque ☐ Celluloid ☐ China ☐ Cloth
☐ Composition ☐ Hard Plastic ☐ Papier-mâché
☐ Vinyl ☐ Wax ☐ Wood ☐ Other _____

Type (check one)

☐ Socket ☐ Flange ☐ Shoulder head
☐ Head on shoulder plate ☐ Other _____

Hair (check one)

☐ Wig (☐ Mohair ☐ Human Hair ☐ Synthetic
☐ Other_____)
☐ Molded Hair ☐ Painted ☐ Other _____
Hair color _____

Eyes (check one)

☐ Glass (☐ Set ☐ Sleeping ☐ Flirty
☐ Paperweight ☐ Threaded)
☐ Decal ☐ Intaglio ☐ Metal ☐ Painted
☐ Eyelashes painted ☐ Hair eyelashes
☐ Synthetic lashes

Mouth (check one)

☐ Closed mouth ☐ Open/Closed ☐ Open mouth
☐ Teeth ☐ Tongue
☐ Other _____

Ears (check one)

☐ Pierced in head ☐ Pierced through lobe
☐ Applied ☐ Other _____

Body (check all appropriate)

☐ Jointed at neck ☐ Elbows ☐ Waist ☐ Wrist
☐ Hips ☐ Knees ☐ Ankles
☐ Other _____

Torso

Material _____

Arms (check one)

☐ Ball jointed ☐ Bent limb ☐ Straight wrist
Material _____

Legs (check one)

☐ Ball jointed ☐ Bent limb ☐ Straight
Material _____

Mark(s) on Body

Where located _____
Stamped, incised: _____
Signed by ☐ Artist ☐ Manufacturer

Clothing (check one)

☐ Original to doll ☐ Contemporary with doll

Replacement clothing made by _____
_____

Outerwear

Style_____
_____

Fabric _____
_____

Color _____

Trim_____

Underwear

Fabric _____
_____

Trim_____

Accessories_____
_____
_____

References

References: (Book magazine article, internet)
Source, author, page# _____
_____
_____

For a similar doll, see:_____
_____
_____

Ribbons & Awards: _____
_____
_____
_____

My Doll Organizer©

Doll # _____

Photo

Head Markings:

Body Markings:

Name of Doll _____

Maker of Doll _____

Height _____

Acquired from _____

    When acquired _____

    Purchase price $_____

    Replacement cost (book value) $_____

    Value (date & source) $_____

    _____

Category/Type of doll _____

Condition _____

_____

_____

Repairs _____

_____

_____

    Done by _____

    Repair date _____

    Repair cost _____

Original box, tags, other _____

_____

_____

Head

Material (check one)
- ☐ Bisque ☐ Celluloid ☐ China ☐ Cloth
- ☐ Composition ☐ Hard Plastic ☐ Papier-mâché
- ☐ Vinyl ☐ Wax ☐ Wood ☐ Other _____

Type (check one)
- ☐ Socket ☐ Flange ☐ Shoulder head
- ☐ Head on shoulder plate ☐ Other _____

Hair (check one)
- ☐ Wig (☐ Mohair ☐ Human Hair ☐ Synthetic
  ☐ Other_____)
- ☐ Molded Hair ☐ Painted ☐ Other _____
- Hair color _____

Eyes (check one)
- ☐ Glass (☐ Set ☐ Sleeping ☐ Flirty
  ☐ Paperweight ☐ Threaded)
- ☐ Decal ☐ Intaglio ☐ Metal ☐ Painted
- ☐ Eyelashes painted ☐ Hair eyelashes
- ☐ Synthetic lashes

Mouth (check one)
- ☐ Closed mouth ☐ Open/Closed ☐ Open mouth
- ☐ Teeth ☐ Tongue
- ☐ Other _____

Ears (check one)
- ☐ Pierced in head ☐ Pierced through lobe
- ☐ Applied ☐ Other _____

Body (check all appropriate)
- ☐ Jointed at neck ☐ Elbows ☐ Waist ☐ Wrist
- ☐ Hips ☐ Knees ☐ Ankles
- ☐ Other _____

Torso
- Material _____

Arms (check one)
- ☐ Ball jointed ☐ Bent limb ☐ Straight wrist
- Material _____

Legs (check one)
- ☐ Ball jointed ☐ Bent limb ☐ Straight
- Material _____

Mark(s) on Body
- Where located _____
- Stamped, incised: _____
- Signed by ☐ Artist ☐ Manufacturer

Clothing (check one)
- ☐ Original to doll ☐ Contemporary with doll

Replacement clothing made by _____
_____

Outerwear
- Style _____
  _____
- Fabric _____
  _____
- Color _____
- Trim _____

Underwear
- Fabric _____
  _____
- Trim _____

Accessories _____
_____

References

References: (Book magazine article, internet)
- Source, author, page# _____
  _____
  _____

For a similar doll, see: _____
_____
_____

Ribbons & Awards: _____
_____
_____
_____

My Doll Organizer©

Doll # _____

Photo

Head Markings:

Body Markings:

Name of Doll _____

Maker of Doll _____

Height _____

Acquired from _____

    When acquired _____

    Purchase price $ _____

    Replacement cost (book value) $_____

    Value (date & source) $_____

    _____

Category/Type of doll _____

Condition _____

Repairs _____

_____

_____

    Done by _____

    Repair date _____

    Repair cost _____

Original box, tags, other _____

_____

_____

_____

Head

Material (check one)
☐ Bisque ☐ Celluloid ☐ China ☐ Cloth
☐ Composition ☐ Hard Plastic ☐ Papier-mâché
☐ Vinyl ☐ Wax ☐ Wood ☐ Other _____

Type (check one)
☐ Socket ☐ Flange ☐ Shoulder head
☐ Head on shoulder plate ☐ Other _____

Hair (check one)
☐ Wig (☐ Mohair ☐ Human Hair ☐ Synthetic
　　　　☐ Other_____)
☐ Molded Hair ☐ Painted ☐ Other _____
Hair color _____

Eyes (check one)
☐ Glass (☐ Set ☐ Sleeping ☐ Flirty
　　　☐ Paperweight ☐ Threaded)
☐ Decal ☐ Intaglio ☐ Metal ☐ Painted
☐ Eyelashes painted ☐ Hair eyelashes
☐ Synthetic lashes

Mouth (check one)
☐ Closed mouth ☐ Open/Closed ☐ Open mouth
☐ Teeth ☐ Tongue
☐ Other _____

Ears (check one)
☐ Pierced in head ☐ Pierced through lobe
☐ Applied ☐ Other _____

Body (check all appropriate)
☐ Jointed at neck ☐ Elbows ☐ Waist ☐ Wrist
☐ Hips ☐ Knees ☐ Ankles
☐ Other _____

Torso
Material _____

Arms (check one)
☐ Ball jointed ☐ Bent limb ☐ Straight wrist
Material _____

Legs (check one)
☐ Ball jointed ☐ Bent limb ☐ Straight
Material _____

Mark(s) on Body
Where located _____
Stamped, incised: _____
Signed by ☐ Artist ☐ Manufacturer

Clothing (check one)
☐ Original to doll ☐ Contemporary with doll

Replacement clothing made by _____
_____

Outerwear
Style_____
_____

Fabric _____
_____

Color _____

Trim_____

Underwear
Fabric _____
_____

Trim_____

Accessories_____
_____
_____

References
References: (Book magazine article, internet)
Source, author, page# _____
_____
_____

For a similar doll, see:_____
_____
_____

Ribbons & Awards: _____
_____
_____
_____

My Doll Organizer©

Doll # _____

Photo

Head Markings:

Body Markings:

Name of Doll _____

Maker of Doll _____

Height _____

Acquired from _____

    When acquired _____

    Purchase price $ _____

    Replacement cost (book value) $ _____

    Value (date & source) $ _____

_____

Category/Type of doll _____

Condition _____

Repairs _____

_____

_____

    Done by _____

    Repair date _____

    Repair cost _____

Original box, tags, other _____

_____

_____

Head

Material (check one)
☐ Bisque ☐ Celluloid ☐ China ☐ Cloth
☐ Composition ☐ Hard Plastic ☐ Papier-mâché
☐ Vinyl ☐ Wax ☐ Wood ☐ Other_____

Type (check one)
☐ Socket ☐ Flange ☐ Shoulder head
☐ Head on shoulder plate ☐ Other_____

Hair (check one)
☐ Wig (☐ Mohair ☐ Human Hair ☐ Synthetic
    ☐ Other_____)
☐ Molded Hair ☐ Painted ☐ Other _____
Hair color _____

Eyes (check one)
☐ Glass (☐ Set ☐ Sleeping ☐ Flirty
    ☐ Paperweight ☐ Threaded)
☐ Decal ☐ Intaglio ☐ Metal ☐ Painted
☐ Eyelashes painted ☐ Hair eyelashes
☐ Synthetic lashes

Mouth (check one)
☐ Closed mouth ☐ Open/Closed ☐ Open mouth
☐ Teeth ☐ Tongue
☐ Other _____

Ears (check one)
☐ Pierced in head ☐ Pierced through lobe
☐ Applied ☐ Other _____

Body (check all appropriate)
☐ Jointed at neck ☐ Elbows ☐ Waist ☐ Wrist
☐ Hips ☐ Knees ☐ Ankles
☐ Other _____

Torso
Material _____

Arms (check one)
☐ Ball jointed ☐ Bent limb ☐ Straight wrist
Material _____

Legs (check one)
☐ Ball jointed ☐ Bent limb ☐ Straight
Material _____

Mark(s) on Body
Where located _____
Stamped, incised: _____
Signed by ☐ Artist ☐ Manufacturer

Clothing (check one)
☐ Original to doll ☐ Contemporary with doll

Replacement clothing made by _____
_____

Outerwear
Style_____
_____

Fabric _____
_____

Color _____

Trim_____

Underwear
Fabric _____
_____

Trim _____

Accessories_____
_____

References
References: (Book magazine article, internet)
Source, author, page# _____
_____
_____

For a similar doll, see:_____
_____
_____

Ribbons & Awards: _____
_____
_____
_____

My Doll Organizer©

Doll # _____

Photo

Head Markings:

Body Markings:

Name of Doll _____

Maker of Doll _____

Height _____

Acquired from _____

    When acquired _____

    Purchase price $ _____

    Replacement cost (book value) $ _____

    Value (date & source) $ _____

_____

Category/Type of doll _____

Condition _____

_____

_____

Repairs _____

_____

_____

_____

    Done by _____

    Repair date _____

    Repair cost _____

Original box, tags, other _____

_____

_____

Head

Material (check one)
☐ Bisque ☐ Celluloid ☐ China ☐ Cloth
☐ Composition ☐ Hard Plastic ☐ Papier-mâché
☐ Vinyl ☐ Wax ☐ Wood ☐ Other_____

Type (check one)
☐ Socket ☐ Flange ☐ Shoulder head
☐ Head on shoulder plate ☐ Other_____

Hair (check one)
☐ Wig (☐ Mohair ☐ Human Hair ☐ Synthetic
　　　☐ Other_____)
☐ Molded Hair ☐ Painted ☐ Other_____
Hair color _____

Eyes (check one)
☐ Glass (☐ Set ☐ Sleeping ☐ Flirty
　　　☐ Paperweight ☐ Threaded)
☐ Decal ☐ Intaglio ☐ Metal ☐ Painted
☐ Eyelashes painted ☐ Hair eyelashes
☐ Synthetic lashes

Mouth (check one)
☐ Closed mouth ☐ Open/Closed ☐ Open mouth
☐ Teeth ☐ Tongue
☐ Other _____

Ears (check one)
☐ Pierced in head ☐ Pierced through lobe
☐ Applied ☐ Other _____

Body (check all appropriate)
☐ Jointed at neck ☐ Elbows ☐ Waist ☐ Wrist
☐ Hips ☐ Knees ☐ Ankles
☐ Other _____

Torso
Material _____

Arms (check one)
☐ Ball jointed ☐ Bent limb ☐ Straight wrist
Material _____

Legs (check one)
☐ Ball jointed ☐ Bent limb ☐ Straight
Material _____

Mark(s) on Body
Where located _____
Stamped, incised: _____
Signed by ☐ Artist ☐ Manufacturer

Clothing (check one)
☐ Original to doll ☐ Contemporary with doll

Replacement clothing made by _____
_____

Outerwear
Style_____
_____

Fabric _____
_____

Color _____

Trim_____

Underwear
Fabric _____
_____

Trim_____

Accessories_____
_____
_____

References
References: (Book magazine article, internet)
Source, author, page# _____
_____
_____

For a similar doll, see:_____
_____
_____

Ribbons & Awards: _____
_____
_____
_____

My Doll Organizer©

Doll # _____

Photo

Head Markings:

Body Markings:

Name of Doll _____

Maker of Doll _____

Height _____

Acquired from _____

    When acquired _____

    Purchase price $_____

    Replacement cost (book value) $_____

    Value (date & source) $_____

    _____

Category/Type of doll _____

Condition _____

_____

Repairs _____

_____

_____

    Done by _____

    Repair date _____

    Repair cost _____

Original box, tags, other _____

_____

Head

Material (check one)
☐ Bisque ☐ Celluloid ☐ China ☐ Cloth
☐ Composition ☐ Hard Plastic ☐ Papier-mâché
☐ Vinyl ☐ Wax ☐ Wood ☐ Other_____

Type (check one)
☐ Socket ☐ Flange ☐ Shoulder head
☐ Head on shoulder plate ☐ Other_____

Hair (check one)
☐ Wig (☐ Mohair ☐ Human Hair ☐ Synthetic
　　　☐ Other_____)
☐ Molded Hair ☐ Painted ☐ Other_____
Hair color _____

Eyes (check one)
☐ Glass (☐ Set ☐ Sleeping ☐ Flirty
　　　☐ Paperweight ☐ Threaded)
☐ Decal ☐ Intaglio ☐ Metal ☐ Painted
☐ Eyelashes painted ☐ Hair eyelashes
☐ Synthetic lashes

Mouth (check one)
☐ Closed mouth ☐ Open/Closed ☐ Open mouth
☐ Teeth ☐ Tongue
☐ Other_____

Ears (check one)
☐ Pierced in head ☐ Pierced through lobe
☐ Applied ☐ Other_____

Body (check all appropriate)
☐ Jointed at neck ☐ Elbows ☐ Waist ☐ Wrist
☐ Hips ☐ Knees ☐ Ankles
☐ Other_____

Torso
Material _____

Arms (check one)
☐ Ball jointed ☐ Bent limb ☐ Straight wrist
Material _____

Legs (check one)
☐ Ball jointed ☐ Bent limb ☐ Straight
Material _____

Mark(s) on Body
Where located _____
Stamped, incised: _____
Signed by ☐ Artist ☐ Manufacturer

Clothing (check one)
☐ Original to doll ☐ Contemporary with doll

Replacement clothing made by _____
_____

Outerwear
Style_____
_____

Fabric _____
_____

Color _____

Trim_____

Underwear
Fabric _____
_____

Trim_____

Accessories_____
_____

References
References: (Book magazine article, internet)
Source, author, page# _____
_____
_____

For a similar doll, see:_____
_____
_____

Ribbons & Awards:_____
_____
_____

My Doll Organizer©

Doll # _____

Photo

Head Markings:

Body Markings:

Name of Doll _____

Maker of Doll _____

Height _____

Acquired from _____

    When acquired _____

    Purchase price $ _____

    Replacement cost (book value) $ _____

    Value (date & source) $ _____

    _____

Category/Type of doll _____

Condition _____

_____

_____

Repairs _____

_____

_____

    Done by _____

    Repair date _____

    Repair cost _____

Original box, tags, other _____

_____

_____

Head

Material (check one)
☐ Bisque ☐ Celluloid ☐ China ☐ Cloth
☐ Composition ☐ Hard Plastic ☐ Papier-mâché
☐ Vinyl ☐ Wax ☐ Wood ☐ Other_____

Type (check one)
☐ Socket ☐ Flange ☐ Shoulder head
☐ Head on shoulder plate ☐ Other_____

Hair (check one)
☐ Wig (☐ Mohair ☐ Human Hair ☐ Synthetic
      ☐ Other_____)
☐ Molded Hair ☐ Painted ☐ Other_____
Hair color _____

Eyes (check one)
☐ Glass (☐ Set ☐ Sleeping ☐ Flirty
      ☐ Paperweight ☐ Threaded)
☐ Decal ☐ Intaglio ☐ Metal ☐ Painted
☐ Eyelashes painted ☐ Hair eyelashes
☐ Synthetic lashes

Mouth (check one)
☐ Closed mouth ☐ Open/Closed ☐ Open mouth
☐ Teeth ☐ Tongue
☐ Other _____

Ears (check one)
☐ Pierced in head ☐ Pierced through lobe
☐ Applied ☐ Other _____

Body (check all appropriate)
☐ Jointed at neck ☐ Elbows ☐ Waist ☐ Wrist
☐ Hips ☐ Knees ☐ Ankles
☐ Other _____

Torso
   Material _____

Arms (check one)
☐ Ball jointed ☐ Bent limb ☐ Straight wrist
   Material _____

Legs (check one)
☐ Ball jointed ☐ Bent limb ☐ Straight
   Material _____

Mark(s) on Body
   Where located _____
   Stamped, incised: _____
   Signed by ☐ Artist ☐ Manufacturer

Clothing (check one)
☐ Original to doll ☐ Contemporary with doll

Replacement clothing made by _____
_____

Outerwear
   Style_____
   _____

   Fabric _____
   _____

   Color _____

   Trim_____

Underwear
   Fabric _____
   _____

   Trim_____

Accessories_____
_____
_____

References
References: (Book magazine article, internet)
   Source, author, page# _____
   _____
   _____

For a similar doll, see:_____
_____
_____

Ribbons & Awards: _____
_____
_____
_____

My Doll Organizer©

Doll # _____

Photo

Head Markings:

Body Markings:

Name of Doll _____

Maker of Doll _____

Height _____

Acquired from _____

    When acquired _____

    Purchase price $ _____

    Replacement cost (book value) $ _____

    Value (date & source) $ _____

                 _____

Category/Type of doll _____

Condition _____

_____

Repairs _____

_____

_____

    Done by _____

    Repair date _____

    Repair cost _____

Original box, tags, other _____

_____

Head

Material (check one)
☐ Bisque ☐ Celluloid ☐ China ☐ Cloth
☐ Composition ☐ Hard Plastic ☐ Papier-mâché
☐ Vinyl ☐ Wax ☐ Wood ☐ Other_____

Type (check one)
☐ Socket ☐ Flange ☐ Shoulder head
☐ Head on shoulder plate ☐ Other_____

Hair (check one)
☐ Wig (☐ Mohair ☐ Human Hair ☐ Synthetic
　　　☐ Other_____)
☐ Molded Hair ☐ Painted ☐ Other_____
Hair color _____

Eyes (check one)
☐ Glass (☐ Set ☐ Sleeping ☐ Flirty
　　　☐ Paperweight ☐ Threaded)
☐ Decal ☐ Intaglio ☐ Metal ☐ Painted
☐ Eyelashes painted ☐ Hair eyelashes
☐ Synthetic lashes

Mouth (check one)
☐ Closed mouth ☐ Open/Closed ☐ Open mouth
☐ Teeth ☐ Tongue
☐ Other _____

Ears (check one)
☐ Pierced in head ☐ Pierced through lobe
☐ Applied ☐ Other _____

Body (check all appropriate)
☐ Jointed at neck ☐ Elbows ☐ Waist ☐ Wrist
☐ Hips ☐ Knees ☐ Ankles
☐ Other _____

Torso
Material _____

Arms (check one)
☐ Ball jointed ☐ Bent limb ☐ Straight wrist
Material _____

Legs (check one)
☐ Ball jointed ☐ Bent limb ☐ Straight
Material _____

Mark(s) on Body
Where located _____
Stamped, incised: _____
Signed by ☐ Artist ☐ Manufacturer

Clothing (check one)
☐ Original to doll ☐ Contemporary with doll

Replacement clothing made by _____
_____

Outerwear
Style_____
_____

Fabric _____
_____

Color _____

Trim_____

Underwear
Fabric _____
_____

Trim _____

Accessories_____
_____

References
References: (Book magazine article, internet)
Source, author, page# _____
_____
_____

For a similar doll, see:_____
_____
_____

Ribbons & Awards: _____
_____
_____
_____

My Doll Organizer©

Doll # _____

Photo

Head Markings:

Body Markings:

Name of Doll _____

Maker of Doll _____

Height _____

Acquired from _____

    When acquired _____

    Purchase price $_____

    Replacement cost (book value) $_____

    Value (date & source) $_____

    _____

Category/Type of doll _____

Condition _____

_____

_____

Repairs _____

_____

_____

    Done by _____

    Repair date _____

    Repair cost _____

Original box, tags, other _____

_____

_____

Head

Material (check one)
☐ Bisque ☐ Celluloid ☐ China ☐ Cloth
☐ Composition ☐ Hard Plastic ☐ Papier-mâché
☐ Vinyl ☐ Wax ☐ Wood ☐ Other_____

Type (check one)
☐ Socket ☐ Flange ☐ Shoulder head
☐ Head on shoulder plate ☐ Other_____

Hair (check one)
☐ Wig (☐ Mohair ☐ Human Hair ☐ Synthetic
    ☐ Other_____)
☐ Molded Hair ☐ Painted ☐ Other _____
Hair color _____

Eyes (check one)
☐ Glass (☐ Set ☐ Sleeping ☐ Flirty
    ☐ Paperweight ☐ Threaded)
☐ Decal ☐ Intaglio ☐ Metal ☐ Painted
☐ Eyelashes painted ☐ Hair eyelashes
☐ Synthetic lashes

Mouth (check one)
☐ Closed mouth ☐ Open/Closed ☐ Open mouth
☐ Teeth ☐ Tongue
☐ Other _____

Ears (check one)
☐ Pierced in head ☐ Pierced through lobe
☐ Applied ☐ Other _____

Body (check all appropriate)
☐ Jointed at neck ☐ Elbows ☐ Waist ☐ Wrist
☐ Hips ☐ Knees ☐ Ankles
☐ Other _____

Torso
Material _____

Arms (check one)
☐ Ball jointed ☐ Bent limb ☐ Straight wrist
Material _____

Legs (check one)
☐ Ball jointed ☐ Bent limb ☐ Straight
Material _____

Mark(s) on Body
Where located _____
Stamped, incised: _____
Signed by ☐ Artist ☐ Manufacturer

Clothing (check one)
☐ Original to doll ☐ Contemporary with doll

Replacement clothing made by_____
_____

Outerwear
Style_____
_____

Fabric _____
_____

Color _____

Trim_____

Underwear
Fabric _____
_____

Trim_____

Accessories_____
_____
_____

References
References: (Book magazine article, internet)
Source, author, page# _____
_____
_____

For a similar doll, see:_____
_____
_____

Ribbons & Awards: _____
_____
_____
_____

My Doll Organizer©

Doll # _____

Photo

Head Markings:

Body Markings:

Name of Doll _____

Maker of Doll _____

Height _____

Acquired from _____

    When acquired _____

    Purchase price $_____

    Replacement cost (book value) $_____

    Value (date & source) $_____

    _____

Category/Type of doll _____

Condition _____

_____

Repairs _____

_____

_____

_____

    Done by _____

    Repair date _____

    Repair cost _____

Original box, tags, other _____

_____

Head

Material (check one)
☐ Bisque ☐ Celluloid ☐ China ☐ Cloth
☐ Composition ☐ Hard Plastic ☐ Papier-mâché
☐ Vinyl ☐ Wax ☐ Wood ☐ Other_____

Type (check one)
☐ Socket ☐ Flange ☐ Shoulder head
☐ Head on shoulder plate ☐ Other_____

Hair (check one)
☐ Wig (☐ Mohair ☐ Human Hair ☐ Synthetic
　　　☐ Other_____)
☐ Molded Hair ☐ Painted ☐ Other_____
Hair color_____

Eyes (check one)
☐ Glass (☐ Set ☐ Sleeping ☐ Flirty
　　　☐ Paperweight ☐ Threaded)
☐ Decal ☐ Intaglio ☐ Metal ☐ Painted
☐ Eyelashes painted ☐ Hair eyelashes
☐ Synthetic lashes

Mouth (check one)
☐ Closed mouth ☐ Open/Closed ☐ Open mouth
☐ Teeth ☐ Tongue
☐ Other_____

Ears (check one)
☐ Pierced in head ☐ Pierced through lobe
☐ Applied ☐ Other_____

Body (check all appropriate)
☐ Jointed at neck ☐ Elbows ☐ Waist ☐ Wrist
☐ Hips ☐ Knees ☐ Ankles
☐ Other_____

Torso
　Material_____

Arms (check one)
☐ Ball jointed ☐ Bent limb ☐ Straight wrist
　Material_____

Legs (check one)
☐ Ball jointed ☐ Bent limb ☐ Straight
　Material_____

Mark(s) on Body
　Where located_____
　Stamped, incised:_____
　Signed by ☐ Artist ☐ Manufacturer

Clothing (check one)
☐ Original to doll ☐ Contemporary with doll

Replacement clothing made by_____
_____

Outerwear
　Style_____
　_____
　Fabric_____
　_____
　Color_____
　Trim_____

Underwear
　Fabric_____
　_____
　Trim_____

Accessories_____
_____

References
References: (Book magazine article, internet)
　Source, author, page#_____
　_____
　_____

For a similar doll, see:_____
_____
_____

Ribbons & Awards:_____
_____
_____
_____

My Doll Organizer©

My Doll Organizer©

Doll # _____

Photo

Head Markings:

Body Markings:

Name of Doll _____

Maker of Doll _____

Height _____

Acquired from _____

    When acquired _____

    Purchase price $_____

    Replacement cost (book value) $_____

    Value (date & source) $_____

                        _____

Category/Type of doll _____

Condition _____

_____

_____

Repairs _____

_____

_____

_____

    Done by _____

    Repair date _____

    Repair cost _____

Original box, tags, other _____

_____

_____

Head

Material (check one)
□ Bisque □ Celluloid □ China □ Cloth
□ Composition □ Hard Plastic □ Papier-mâché
□ Vinyl □ Wax □ Wood □ Other_____

Type (check one)
□ Socket □ Flange □ Shoulder head
□ Head on shoulder plate □ Other_____

Hair (check one)
□ Wig (□ Mohair □ Human Hair □ Synthetic
□ Other_____)
□ Molded Hair □ Painted □ Other_____
Hair color_____

Eyes (check one)
□ Glass (□ Set □ Sleeping □ Flirty
□ Paperweight □ Threaded)
□ Decal □ Intaglio □ Metal □ Painted
□ Eyelashes painted □ Hair eyelashes
□ Synthetic lashes

Mouth (check one)
□ Closed mouth □ Open/Closed □ Open mouth
□ Teeth □ Tongue
□ Other_____

Ears (check one)
□ Pierced in head □ Pierced through lobe
□ Applied □ Other_____

Body (check all appropriate)
□ Jointed at neck □ Elbows □ Waist □ Wrist
□ Hips □ Knees □ Ankles
□ Other_____

Torso
Material_____

Arms (check one)
□ Ball jointed □ Bent limb □ Straight wrist
Material_____

Legs (check one)
□ Ball jointed □ Bent limb □ Straight
Material_____

Mark(s) on Body
Where located_____
Stamped, incised:_____
Signed by □ Artist □ Manufacturer

Clothing (check one)
□ Original to doll □ Contemporary with doll

Replacement clothing made by_____
_____

Outerwear
Style_____
_____

Fabric_____
_____

Color_____

Trim_____

Underwear
Fabric_____
_____

Trim_____

Accessories_____
_____
_____

References
References: (Book magazine article, internet)
Source, author, page#_____
_____
_____

For a similar doll, see:_____
_____
_____

Ribbons & Awards:_____
_____
_____
_____

My Doll Organizer©

Doll # _____

Photo

Head Markings:

Body Markings:

Name of Doll _____

Maker of Doll _____

Height _____

Acquired from _____

    When acquired _____

    Purchase price $_____

    Replacement cost (book value) $_____

    Value (date & source) $_____

_____

Category/Type of doll _____

Condition _____

_____

Repairs _____

_____

_____

    Done by _____

    Repair date _____

    Repair cost _____

Original box, tags, other _____

_____

Head

Material (check one)
☐ Bisque ☐ Celluloid ☐ China ☐ Cloth
☐ Composition ☐ Hard Plastic ☐ Papier-mâché
☐ Vinyl ☐ Wax ☐ Wood ☐ Other _____

Type (check one)
☐ Socket ☐ Flange ☐ Shoulder head
☐ Head on shoulder plate ☐ Other _____

Hair (check one)
☐ Wig (☐ Mohair ☐ Human Hair ☐ Synthetic
　　☐ Other _____)
☐ Molded Hair ☐ Painted ☐ Other _____
Hair color _____

Eyes (check one)
☐ Glass (☐ Set ☐ Sleeping ☐ Flirty
　　☐ Paperweight ☐ Threaded)
☐ Decal ☐ Intaglio ☐ Metal ☐ Painted
☐ Eyelashes painted ☐ Hair eyelashes
☐ Synthetic lashes

Mouth (check one)
☐ Closed mouth ☐ Open/Closed ☐ Open mouth
☐ Teeth ☐ Tongue
☐ Other _____

Ears (check one)
☐ Pierced in head ☐ Pierced through lobe
☐ Applied ☐ Other _____

Body (check all appropriate)
☐ Jointed at neck ☐ Elbows ☐ Waist ☐ Wrist
☐ Hips ☐ Knees ☐ Ankles
☐ Other _____

Torso
　Material _____

Arms (check one)
☐ Ball jointed ☐ Bent limb ☐ Straight wrist
　Material _____

Legs (check one)
☐ Ball jointed ☐ Bent limb ☐ Straight
　Material _____

Mark(s) on Body
　Where located _____
　Stamped, incised: _____
　Signed by ☐ Artist ☐ Manufacturer

Clothing (check one)
☐ Original to doll ☐ Contemporary with doll

Replacement clothing made by _____
_____

Outerwear
　Style _____
　_____

　Fabric _____
　_____

　Color _____

　Trim _____

Underwear
　Fabric _____
　_____

　Trim _____

Accessories _____
_____
_____

References
References: (Book magazine article, internet)
　Source, author, page# _____
　_____
　_____

For a similar doll, see: _____
_____
_____

Ribbons & Awards: _____
_____
_____
_____

My Doll Organizer©

Doll # _____

Photo

Head Markings:

Body Markings:

Name of Doll _____

Maker of Doll _____

Height _____

Acquired from _____

    When acquired _____

    Purchase price $ _____

    Replacement cost (book value) $ _____

    Value (date & source) $ _____

                  _____

Category/Type of doll _____

Condition _____

_____

_____

Repairs _____

_____

_____

    Done by _____

    Repair date _____

    Repair cost _____

Original box, tags, other _____

_____

_____

Head

Material (check one)

☐ Bisque ☐ Celluloid ☐ China ☐ Cloth
☐ Composition ☐ Hard Plastic ☐ Papier-mâché
☐ Vinyl ☐ Wax ☐ Wood ☐ Other _____

Type (check one)

☐ Socket ☐ Flange ☐ Shoulder head
☐ Head on shoulder plate ☐ Other _____

Hair (check one)

☐ Wig (☐ Mohair ☐ Human Hair ☐ Synthetic
☐ Other_____)
☐ Molded Hair ☐ Painted ☐ Other _____
Hair color _____

Eyes (check one)

☐ Glass (☐ Set ☐ Sleeping ☐ Flirty
☐ Paperweight ☐ Threaded)
☐ Decal ☐ Intaglio ☐ Metal ☐ Painted
☐ Eyelashes painted ☐ Hair eyelashes
☐ Synthetic lashes

Mouth (check one)

☐ Closed mouth ☐ Open/Closed ☐ Open mouth
☐ Teeth ☐ Tongue
☐ Other _____

Ears (check one)

☐ Pierced in head ☐ Pierced through lobe
☐ Applied ☐ Other _____

Body (check all appropriate)

☐ Jointed at neck ☐ Elbows ☐ Waist ☐ Wrist
☐ Hips ☐ Knees ☐ Ankles
☐ Other _____

Torso

Material _____

Arms (check one)

☐ Ball jointed ☐ Bent limb ☐ Straight wrist
Material _____

Legs (check one)

☐ Ball jointed ☐ Bent limb ☐ Straight
Material _____

Mark(s) on Body

Where located _____
Stamped, incised: _____
Signed by ☐ Artist ☐ Manufacturer

Clothing (check one)

☐ Original to doll ☐ Contemporary with doll

Replacement clothing made by _____
_____

Outerwear

Style_____
_____

Fabric _____
_____

Color _____

Trim_____

Underwear

Fabric _____
_____

Trim_____

Accessories_____
_____
_____

References

References: (Book magazine article, internet)
Source, author, page# _____
_____
_____

For a similar doll, see:_____
_____
_____

Ribbons & Awards: _____
_____
_____

My Doll Organizer©

Doll # _____

Photo

Head Markings:

Body Markings:

Name of Doll _____

Maker of Doll _____

Height _____

Acquired from _____

    When acquired _____

    Purchase price $_____

    Replacement cost (book value) $_____

    Value (date & source) $_____

    _____

Category/Type of doll _____

Condition _____

Repairs _____

_____

_____

    Done by _____

    Repair date _____

    Repair cost _____

Original box, tags, other _____

_____

_____

Head

Material (check one)
☐ Bisque ☐ Celluloid ☐ China ☐ Cloth
☐ Composition ☐ Hard Plastic ☐ Papier-mâché
☐ Vinyl ☐ Wax ☐ Wood ☐ Other_____

Type (check one)
☐ Socket ☐ Flange ☐ Shoulder head
☐ Head on shoulder plate ☐ Other_____

Hair (check one)
☐ Wig (☐ Mohair ☐ Human Hair ☐ Synthetic
        ☐ Other_____)
☐ Molded Hair ☐ Painted ☐ Other_____
Hair color_____

Eyes (check one)
☐ Glass (☐ Set ☐ Sleeping ☐ Flirty
        ☐ Paperweight ☐ Threaded)
☐ Decal ☐ Intaglio ☐ Metal ☐ Painted
☐ Eyelashes painted ☐ Hair eyelashes
☐ Synthetic lashes

Mouth (check one)
☐ Closed mouth ☐ Open/Closed ☐ Open mouth
☐ Teeth ☐ Tongue
☐ Other_____

Ears (check one)
☐ Pierced in head ☐ Pierced through lobe
☐ Applied ☐ Other_____

Body (check all appropriate)
☐ Jointed at neck ☐ Elbows ☐ Waist ☐ Wrist
☐ Hips ☐ Knees ☐ Ankles
☐ Other_____

Torso
    Material_____

Arms (check one)
☐ Ball jointed ☐ Bent limb ☐ Straight wrist
    Material_____

Legs (check one)
☐ Ball jointed ☐ Bent limb ☐ Straight
    Material_____

Mark(s) on Body
    Where located_____
    Stamped, incised:_____
    Signed by ☐ Artist ☐ Manufacturer

Clothing (check one)
☐ Original to doll ☐ Contemporary with doll

Replacement clothing made by_____
_____

Outerwear
    Style_____
    _____

    Fabric_____
    _____

    Color_____

    Trim_____

Underwear
    Fabric_____
    _____

    Trim_____

Accessories_____
_____
_____

References
References: (Book magazine article, internet)
    Source, author, page#_____
    _____
    _____

For a similar doll, see:_____
_____
_____

Ribbons & Awards:_____
_____
_____
_____

My Doll Organizer©

My Doll Organizer©

Doll # _____

Photo

Head Markings:

Body Markings:

Name of Doll _____

Maker of Doll _____

Height _____

Acquired from _____

　　When acquired _____

　　Purchase price $ _____

　　Replacement cost (book value) $_____

　　Value (date & source) $_____

　　_____

Category/Type of doll _____

Condition _____

_____

_____

Repairs _____

_____

_____

_____

　　Done by _____

　　Repair date _____

　　Repair cost _____

Original box, tags, other _____

_____

_____

© 2000 Hobby House Press, Inc.

Head

Material (check one)
- ☐ Bisque ☐ Celluloid ☐ China ☐ Cloth
- ☐ Composition ☐ Hard Plastic ☐ Papier-mâché
- ☐ Vinyl ☐ Wax ☐ Wood ☐ Other_____

Type (check one)
- ☐ Socket ☐ Flange ☐ Shoulder head
- ☐ Head on shoulder plate ☐ Other_____

Hair (check one)
- ☐ Wig (☐ Mohair ☐ Human Hair ☐ Synthetic
  ☐ Other_____)
- ☐ Molded Hair ☐ Painted ☐ Other _____
- Hair color _____

Eyes (check one)
- ☐ Glass (☐ Set ☐ Sleeping ☐ Flirty
  ☐ Paperweight ☐ Threaded)
- ☐ Decal ☐ Intaglio ☐ Metal ☐ Painted
- ☐ Eyelashes painted ☐ Hair eyelashes
- ☐ Synthetic lashes

Mouth (check one)
- ☐ Closed mouth ☐ Open/Closed ☐ Open mouth
- ☐ Teeth ☐ Tongue
- ☐ Other _____

Ears (check one)
- ☐ Pierced in head ☐ Pierced through lobe
- ☐ Applied ☐ Other _____

Body (check all appropriate)
- ☐ Jointed at neck ☐ Elbows ☐ Waist ☐ Wrist
- ☐ Hips ☐ Knees ☐ Ankles
- ☐ Other _____

Torso
- Material _____

Arms (check one)
- ☐ Ball jointed ☐ Bent limb ☐ Straight wrist
- Material _____

Legs (check one)
- ☐ Ball jointed ☐ Bent limb ☐ Straight
- Material _____

Mark(s) on Body
- Where located _____
- Stamped, incised: _____
- Signed by ☐ Artist ☐ Manufacturer

Clothing (check one)
☐ Original to doll ☐ Contemporary with doll

Replacement clothing made by _____
_____

Outerwear
- Style_____
  _____
- Fabric _____
  _____
- Color _____
- Trim_____

Underwear
- Fabric _____
  _____
- Trim_____

Accessories_____
_____
_____

References
References: (Book magazine article, internet)
- Source, author, page# _____
  _____
  _____
  _____

For a similar doll, see:_____
_____
_____
_____

Ribbons & Awards: _____
_____
_____
_____

My Doll Organizer©

Doll # _____

Photo

Head Markings:

Body Markings:

Name of Doll _____

Maker of Doll _____

Height _____

Acquired from _____

    When acquired _____

    Purchase price $_____

    Replacement cost (book value) $_____

    Value (date & source) $_____

    _____

Category/Type of doll _____

Condition _____

_____

_____

Repairs _____

_____

_____

    Done by _____

    Repair date _____

    Repair cost _____

Original box, tags, other _____

_____

_____

Head

Material (check one)
- ☐ Bisque ☐ Celluloid ☐ China ☐ Cloth
- ☐ Composition ☐ Hard Plastic ☐ Papier-mâché
- ☐ Vinyl ☐ Wax ☐ Wood ☐ Other _____

Type (check one)
- ☐ Socket ☐ Flange ☐ Shoulder head
- ☐ Head on shoulder plate ☐ Other _____

Hair (check one)
- ☐ Wig (☐ Mohair ☐ Human Hair ☐ Synthetic
     ☐ Other_____)
- ☐ Molded Hair ☐ Painted ☐ Other _____
- Hair color _____

Eyes (check one)
- ☐ Glass (☐ Set ☐ Sleeping ☐ Flirty
     ☐ Paperweight ☐ Threaded)
- ☐ Decal ☐ Intaglio ☐ Metal ☐ Painted
- ☐ Eyelashes painted ☐ Hair eyelashes
- ☐ Synthetic lashes

Mouth (check one)
- ☐ Closed mouth ☐ Open/Closed ☐ Open mouth
- ☐ Teeth ☐ Tongue
- ☐ Other _____

Ears (check one)
- ☐ Pierced in head ☐ Pierced through lobe
- ☐ Applied ☐ Other _____

Body (check all appropriate)
- ☐ Jointed at neck ☐ Elbows ☐ Waist ☐ Wrist
- ☐ Hips ☐ Knees ☐ Ankles
- ☐ Other _____

Torso
- Material _____

Arms (check one)
- ☐ Ball jointed ☐ Bent limb ☐ Straight wrist
- Material _____

Legs (check one)
- ☐ Ball jointed ☐ Bent limb ☐ Straight
- Material _____

Mark(s) on Body
- Where located _____
- Stamped, incised: _____
- Signed by ☐ Artist ☐ Manufacturer

Clothing (check one)
- ☐ Original to doll ☐ Contemporary with doll

Replacement clothing made by _____
_____

Outerwear
- Style _____
  _____
- Fabric _____
  _____
- Color _____
- Trim _____

Underwear
- Fabric _____
  _____
- Trim _____

Accessories _____
_____
_____

References
References: (Book magazine article, internet)
- Source, author, page# _____
  _____
  _____

For a similar doll, see: _____
_____
_____

Ribbons & Awards: _____
_____
_____
_____

My Doll Organizer©

Doll # _____

Photo

Head Markings:

Body Markings:

Name of Doll _____

Maker of Doll _____

Height _____

Acquired from _____

    When acquired _____

    Purchase price $ _____

    Replacement cost (book value) $_____

    Value (date & source) $_____

    _____

Category/Type of doll _____

Condition _____

_____

_____

Repairs _____

_____

_____

_____

    Done by _____

    Repair date _____

    Repair cost _____

Original box, tags, other _____

_____

_____

Head

Material (check one)
- ☐ Bisque ☐ Celluloid ☐ China ☐ Cloth
- ☐ Composition ☐ Hard Plastic ☐ Papier-mâché
- ☐ Vinyl ☐ Wax ☐ Wood ☐ Other _____

Type (check one)
- ☐ Socket ☐ Flange ☐ Shoulder head
- ☐ Head on shoulder plate ☐ Other _____

Hair (check one)
- ☐ Wig (☐ Mohair ☐ Human Hair ☐ Synthetic
  - ☐ Other_____)
- ☐ Molded Hair ☐ Painted ☐ Other _____
- Hair color _____

Eyes (check one)
- ☐ Glass (☐ Set ☐ Sleeping ☐ Flirty
  - ☐ Paperweight ☐ Threaded)
- ☐ Decal ☐ Intaglio ☐ Metal ☐ Painted
- ☐ Eyelashes painted ☐ Hair eyelashes
- ☐ Synthetic lashes

Mouth (check one)
- ☐ Closed mouth ☐ Open/Closed ☐ Open mouth
- ☐ Teeth ☐ Tongue
- ☐ Other _____

Ears (check one)
- ☐ Pierced in head ☐ Pierced through lobe
- ☐ Applied ☐ Other _____

Body (check all appropriate)
- ☐ Jointed at neck ☐ Elbows ☐ Waist ☐ Wrist
- ☐ Hips ☐ Knees ☐ Ankles
- ☐ Other _____

Torso
- Material _____

Arms (check one)
- ☐ Ball jointed ☐ Bent limb ☐ Straight wrist
- Material _____

Legs (check one)
- ☐ Ball jointed ☐ Bent limb ☐ Straight
- Material _____

Mark(s) on Body
- Where located _____
- Stamped, incised: _____
- Signed by ☐ Artist ☐ Manufacturer

Clothing (check one)
- ☐ Original to doll ☐ Contemporary with doll

Replacement clothing made by _____
_____

Outerwear
- Style_____
- _____
- Fabric _____
- _____
- Color _____
- Trim_____

Underwear
- Fabric _____
- _____
- Trim_____

Accessories_____
_____
_____

References
References: (Book magazine article, internet)
- Source, author, page# _____
- _____
- _____
- _____

For a similar doll, see:_____
_____
_____
_____

Ribbons & Awards: _____
_____
_____
_____

My Doll Organizer©

Doll # _____

Photo

Head Markings:

Body Markings:

Name of Doll _____

Maker of Doll _____

Height _____

Acquired from _____

    When acquired _____

    Purchase price $_____

    Replacement cost (book value) $_____

    Value (date & source) $_____

    _____

Category/Type of doll _____

Condition _____

_____

_____

Repairs _____

_____

_____

_____

    Done by _____

    Repair date _____

    Repair cost _____

Original box, tags, other _____

_____

_____

Head

Material (check one)
☐ Bisque ☐ Celluloid ☐ China ☐ Cloth
☐ Composition ☐ Hard Plastic ☐ Papier-mâché
☐ Vinyl ☐ Wax ☐ Wood ☐ Other _____

Type (check one)
☐ Socket ☐ Flange ☐ Shoulder head
☐ Head on shoulder plate ☐ Other _____

Hair (check one)
☐ Wig (☐ Mohair ☐ Human Hair ☐ Synthetic
       ☐ Other_____)
☐ Molded Hair ☐ Painted ☐ Other _____
Hair color _____

Eyes (check one)
☐ Glass (☐ Set ☐ Sleeping ☐ Flirty
       ☐ Paperweight ☐ Threaded)
☐ Decal ☐ Intaglio ☐ Metal ☐ Painted
☐ Eyelashes painted ☐ Hair eyelashes
☐ Synthetic lashes

Mouth (check one)
☐ Closed mouth ☐ Open/Closed ☐ Open mouth
☐ Teeth ☐ Tongue
☐ Other _____

Ears (check one)
☐ Pierced in head ☐ Pierced through lobe
☐ Applied ☐ Other _____

Body (check all appropriate)
☐ Jointed at neck ☐ Elbows ☐ Waist ☐ Wrist
☐ Hips ☐ Knees ☐ Ankles
☐ Other _____

Torso
Material _____

Arms (check one)
☐ Ball jointed ☐ Bent limb ☐ Straight wrist
Material _____

Legs (check one)
☐ Ball jointed ☐ Bent limb ☐ Straight
Material _____

Mark(s) on Body
Where located _____
Stamped, incised: _____
Signed by ☐ Artist ☐ Manufacturer

Clothing (check one)
☐ Original to doll ☐ Contemporary with doll

Replacement clothing made by _____
_____

Outerwear
Style _____
_____

Fabric _____
_____

Color _____

Trim _____

Underwear
Fabric _____
_____

Trim _____

Accessories _____
_____
_____

References
References: (Book magazine article, internet)
Source, author, page# _____
_____
_____

For a similar doll, see: _____
_____
_____

Ribbons & Awards: _____
_____
_____
_____

My Doll Organizer©

Doll # _____

Photo

Head Markings:

Body Markings:

Name of Doll _____

Maker of Doll _____

Height _____

Acquired from _____

　　When acquired _____

　　Purchase price $_____

　　Replacement cost (book value) $_____

　　Value (date & source) $_____

　　_____

Category/Type of doll _____

Condition _____

_____

_____

Repairs _____

_____

_____

_____

　　Done by _____

　　Repair date _____

　　Repair cost _____

Original box, tags, other _____

_____

_____

Head

Material (check one)
☐ Bisque ☐ Celluloid ☐ China ☐ Cloth
☐ Composition ☐ Hard Plastic ☐ Papier-mâché
☐ Vinyl ☐ Wax ☐ Wood ☐ Other _____

Type (check one)
☐ Socket ☐ Flange ☐ Shoulder head
☐ Head on shoulder plate ☐ Other _____

Hair (check one)
☐ Wig (☐ Mohair ☐ Human Hair ☐ Synthetic
☐ Other_____)
☐ Molded Hair ☐ Painted ☐ Other _____
Hair color _____

Eyes (check one)
☐ Glass (☐ Set ☐ Sleeping ☐ Flirty
☐ Paperweight ☐ Threaded)
☐ Decal ☐ Intaglio ☐ Metal ☐ Painted
☐ Eyelashes painted ☐ Hair eyelashes
☐ Synthetic lashes

Mouth (check one)
☐ Closed mouth ☐ Open/Closed ☐ Open mouth
☐ Teeth ☐ Tongue
☐ Other _____

Ears (check one)
☐ Pierced in head ☐ Pierced through lobe
☐ Applied ☐ Other _____

Body (check all appropriate)
☐ Jointed at neck ☐ Elbows ☐ Waist ☐ Wrist
☐ Hips ☐ Knees ☐ Ankles
☐ Other _____

Torso
Material _____

Arms (check one)
☐ Ball jointed ☐ Bent limb ☐ Straight wrist
Material _____

Legs (check one)
☐ Ball jointed ☐ Bent limb ☐ Straight
Material _____

Mark(s) on Body
Where located _____
Stamped, incised: _____
Signed by ☐ Artist ☐ Manufacturer

Clothing (check one)
☐ Original to doll ☐ Contemporary with doll

Replacement clothing made by _____
_____

Outerwear
Style _____
_____
Fabric _____
_____
Color _____
Trim _____

Underwear
Fabric _____
_____
Trim _____

Accessories _____
_____
_____

References
References: (Book magazine article, internet)
Source, author, page# _____
_____
_____

For a similar doll, see: _____
_____
_____

Ribbons & Awards: _____
_____
_____
_____

My Doll Organizer©

Doll # _____

Photo

Head Markings:

Body Markings:

Name of Doll _____

Maker of Doll _____

Height _____

Acquired from _____

   When acquired _____

   Purchase price $ _____

   Replacement cost (book value) $ _____

   Value (date & source) $ _____

                _____

Category/Type of doll _____

Condition _____

_____

_____

Repairs _____

_____

_____

_____

   Done by _____

   Repair date _____

   Repair cost _____

Original box, tags, other _____

_____

_____

Head

Material (check one)
☐ Bisque ☐ Celluloid ☐ China ☐ Cloth
☐ Composition ☐ Hard Plastic ☐ Papier-mâché
☐ Vinyl ☐ Wax ☐ Wood ☐ Other_____

Type (check one)
☐ Socket ☐ Flange ☐ Shoulder head
☐ Head on shoulder plate ☐ Other_____

Hair (check one)
☐ Wig (☐ Mohair ☐ Human Hair ☐ Synthetic
　　　☐ Other_____)
☐ Molded Hair ☐ Painted ☐ Other_____
Hair color_____

Eyes (check one)
☐ Glass (☐ Set ☐ Sleeping ☐ Flirty
　　　☐ Paperweight ☐ Threaded)
☐ Decal ☐ Intaglio ☐ Metal ☐ Painted
☐ Eyelashes painted ☐ Hair eyelashes
☐ Synthetic lashes

Mouth (check one)
☐ Closed mouth ☐ Open/Closed ☐ Open mouth
☐ Teeth ☐ Tongue
☐ Other_____

Ears (check one)
☐ Pierced in head ☐ Pierced through lobe
☐ Applied ☐ Other_____

Body (check all appropriate)
☐ Jointed at neck ☐ Elbows ☐ Waist ☐ Wrist
☐ Hips ☐ Knees ☐ Ankles
☐ Other_____

Torso
Material_____

Arms (check one)
☐ Ball jointed ☐ Bent limb ☐ Straight wrist
Material_____

Legs (check one)
☐ Ball jointed ☐ Bent limb ☐ Straight
Material_____

Mark(s) on Body
Where located_____
Stamped, incised:_____
Signed by ☐ Artist ☐ Manufacturer

Clothing (check one)
☐ Original to doll ☐ Contemporary with doll

Replacement clothing made by_____
_____

Outerwear
Style_____
_____

Fabric_____
_____

Color_____

Trim_____

Underwear
Fabric_____
_____

Trim_____

Accessories_____
_____

References
References: (Book magazine article, internet)
Source, author, page#_____
_____
_____

For a similar doll, see:_____
_____
_____

Ribbons & Awards:_____
_____
_____
_____

My Doll Organizer©

Doll # _____

Photo

Head Markings:

Body Markings:

Name of Doll _____

Maker of Doll _____

Height _____

Acquired from _____

    When acquired _____

    Purchase price $ _____

    Replacement cost (book value) $_____

    Value (date & source) $_____

    _____

Category/Type of doll _____

Condition _____

_____

_____

Repairs _____

_____

_____

    Done by _____

    Repair date _____

    Repair cost _____

Original box, tags, other _____

_____

_____

© 2000 Hobby House Press, Inc.

Head

Material (check one)
- ☐ Bisque ☐ Celluloid ☐ China ☐ Cloth
- ☐ Composition ☐ Hard Plastic ☐ Papier-mâché
- ☐ Vinyl ☐ Wax ☐ Wood ☐ Other _____

Type (check one)
- ☐ Socket ☐ Flange ☐ Shoulder head
- ☐ Head on shoulder plate ☐ Other _____

Hair (check one)
- ☐ Wig (☐ Mohair ☐ Human Hair ☐ Synthetic
    ☐ Other_____)
- ☐ Molded Hair ☐ Painted ☐ Other _____
- Hair color _____

Eyes (check one)
- ☐ Glass (☐ Set ☐ Sleeping ☐ Flirty
    ☐ Paperweight ☐ Threaded)
- ☐ Decal ☐ Intaglio ☐ Metal ☐ Painted
- ☐ Eyelashes painted ☐ Hair eyelashes
- ☐ Synthetic lashes

Mouth (check one)
- ☐ Closed mouth ☐ Open/Closed ☐ Open mouth
- ☐ Teeth ☐ Tongue
- ☐ Other _____

Ears (check one)
- ☐ Pierced in head ☐ Pierced through lobe
- ☐ Applied ☐ Other _____

Body (check all appropriate)
- ☐ Jointed at neck ☐ Elbows ☐ Waist ☐ Wrist
- ☐ Hips ☐ Knees ☐ Ankles
- ☐ Other _____

Torso
- Material _____

Arms (check one)
- ☐ Ball jointed ☐ Bent limb ☐ Straight wrist
- Material _____

Legs (check one)
- ☐ Ball jointed ☐ Bent limb ☐ Straight
- Material _____

Mark(s) on Body
- Where located _____
- Stamped, incised: _____
- Signed by ☐ Artist ☐ Manufacturer

Clothing (check one)
☐ Original to doll ☐ Contemporary with doll

Replacement clothing made by _____
_____

Outerwear
- Style _____
    _____
- Fabric _____
    _____
- Color _____
- Trim _____

Underwear
- Fabric _____
    _____
- Trim _____

Accessories _____
_____

References
References: (Book magazine article, internet)
- Source, author, page# _____
    _____
    _____

For a similar doll, see: _____
_____
_____

Ribbons & Awards: _____
_____
_____
_____

My Doll Organizer©

Doll # _____

Photo

Head Markings:

Body Markings:

Name of Doll _____

Maker of Doll _____

Height _____

Acquired from _____

    When acquired _____

    Purchase price $ _____

    Replacement cost (book value) $ _____

    Value (date & source) $ _____

                        _____

Category/Type of doll _____

Condition _____

Repairs _____

_____

_____

_____

    Done by _____

    Repair date _____

    Repair cost _____

Original box, tags, other _____

_____

_____

Head

Material (check one)
- ☐ Bisque ☐ Celluloid ☐ China ☐ Cloth
- ☐ Composition ☐ Hard Plastic ☐ Papier-mâché
- ☐ Vinyl ☐ Wax ☐ Wood ☐ Other_____

Type (check one)
- ☐ Socket ☐ Flange ☐ Shoulder head
- ☐ Head on shoulder plate ☐ Other_____

Hair (check one)
- ☐ Wig (☐ Mohair ☐ Human Hair ☐ Synthetic
  - ☐ Other_____)
- ☐ Molded Hair ☐ Painted ☐ Other_____
- Hair color _____

Eyes (check one)
- ☐ Glass (☐ Set ☐ Sleeping ☐ Flirty
  - ☐ Paperweight ☐ Threaded)
- ☐ Decal ☐ Intaglio ☐ Metal ☐ Painted
- ☐ Eyelashes painted ☐ Hair eyelashes
- ☐ Synthetic lashes

Mouth (check one)
- ☐ Closed mouth ☐ Open/Closed ☐ Open mouth
- ☐ Teeth ☐ Tongue
- ☐ Other _____

Ears (check one)
- ☐ Pierced in head ☐ Pierced through lobe
- ☐ Applied ☐ Other _____

Body (check all appropriate)
- ☐ Jointed at neck ☐ Elbows ☐ Waist ☐ Wrist
- ☐ Hips ☐ Knees ☐ Ankles
- ☐ Other _____

Torso
- Material _____

Arms (check one)
- ☐ Ball jointed ☐ Bent limb ☐ Straight wrist
- Material _____

Legs (check one)
- ☐ Ball jointed ☐ Bent limb ☐ Straight
- Material _____

Mark(s) on Body
- Where located _____
- Stamped, incised: _____
- Signed by ☐ Artist ☐ Manufacturer

Clothing (check one)
- ☐ Original to doll ☐ Contemporary with doll

Replacement clothing made by _____
_____

Outerwear
- Style_____
- _____
- Fabric _____
- _____
- Color _____
- Trim_____

Underwear
- Fabric _____
- _____
- Trim _____

Accessories_____
_____

References
References: (Book magazine article, internet)
- Source, author, page# _____
- _____
- _____

For a similar doll, see:_____
_____
_____

Ribbons & Awards: _____
_____
_____
_____

My Doll Organizer©

Doll # _____

Photo

Head Markings:

Body Markings:

Name of Doll _____

Maker of Doll _____

Height _____

Acquired from _____

    When acquired _____

    Purchase price $ _____

    Replacement cost (book value) $ _____

    Value (date & source) $ _____

    _____

Category/Type of doll _____

Condition _____

_____

_____

Repairs _____

_____

_____

_____

    Done by _____

    Repair date _____

    Repair cost _____

Original box, tags, other _____

_____

_____

Head

Material (check one)
- ☐ Bisque ☐ Celluloid ☐ China ☐ Cloth
- ☐ Composition ☐ Hard Plastic ☐ Papier-mâché
- ☐ Vinyl ☐ Wax ☐ Wood ☐ Other_____

Type (check one)
- ☐ Socket ☐ Flange ☐ Shoulder head
- ☐ Head on shoulder plate ☐ Other_____

Hair (check one)
- ☐ Wig (☐ Mohair ☐ Human Hair ☐ Synthetic
  - ☐ Other_____)
- ☐ Molded Hair ☐ Painted ☐ Other_____
- Hair color _____

Eyes (check one)
- ☐ Glass (☐ Set ☐ Sleeping ☐ Flirty
  - ☐ Paperweight ☐ Threaded)
- ☐ Decal ☐ Intaglio ☐ Metal ☐ Painted
- ☐ Eyelashes painted ☐ Hair eyelashes
- ☐ Synthetic lashes

Mouth (check one)
- ☐ Closed mouth ☐ Open/Closed ☐ Open mouth
- ☐ Teeth ☐ Tongue
- ☐ Other_____

Ears (check one)
- ☐ Pierced in head ☐ Pierced through lobe
- ☐ Applied ☐ Other_____

Body (check all appropriate)
- ☐ Jointed at neck ☐ Elbows ☐ Waist ☐ Wrist
- ☐ Hips ☐ Knees ☐ Ankles
- ☐ Other_____

Torso
- Material _____

Arms (check one)
- ☐ Ball jointed ☐ Bent limb ☐ Straight wrist
- Material _____

Legs (check one)
- ☐ Ball jointed ☐ Bent limb ☐ Straight
- Material _____

Mark(s) on Body
- Where located _____
- Stamped, incised: _____
- Signed by ☐ Artist ☐ Manufacturer

Clothing (check one)
- ☐ Original to doll ☐ Contemporary with doll

Replacement clothing made by _____
_____

Outerwear
- Style_____
  - _____
- Fabric _____
  - _____
- Color _____
- Trim_____

Underwear
- Fabric _____
  - _____
- Trim_____

Accessories_____
_____
_____

References

References: (Book magazine article, internet)
- Source, author, page# _____
  - _____
  - _____

For a similar doll, see:_____
_____
_____

Ribbons & Awards: _____
_____
_____
_____

My Doll Organizer©

Doll # _____

Photo

Head Markings:

Body Markings:

Name of Doll _____

Maker of Doll _____

Height _____

Acquired from _____

    When acquired _____

    Purchase price $_____

    Replacement cost (book value) $_____

    Value (date & source) $_____

    _____

Category/Type of doll _____

Condition _____

Repairs _____

_____

_____

    Done by _____

    Repair date _____

    Repair cost _____

Original box, tags, other _____

_____

_____

Head

Material (check one)
☐ Bisque ☐ Celluloid ☐ China ☐ Cloth
☐ Composition ☐ Hard Plastic ☐ Papier-mâché
☐ Vinyl ☐ Wax ☐ Wood ☐ Other _____

Type (check one)
☐ Socket ☐ Flange ☐ Shoulder head
☐ Head on shoulder plate ☐ Other _____

Hair (check one)
☐ Wig (☐ Mohair ☐ Human Hair ☐ Synthetic
       ☐ Other_____)
☐ Molded Hair ☐ Painted ☐ Other _____
Hair color _____

Eyes (check one)
☐ Glass (☐ Set ☐ Sleeping ☐ Flirty
        ☐ Paperweight ☐ Threaded)
☐ Decal ☐ Intaglio ☐ Metal ☐ Painted
☐ Eyelashes painted ☐ Hair eyelashes
☐ Synthetic lashes

Mouth (check one)
☐ Closed mouth ☐ Open/Closed ☐ Open mouth
☐ Teeth ☐ Tongue
☐ Other _____

Ears (check one)
☐ Pierced in head ☐ Pierced through lobe
☐ Applied ☐ Other _____

Body (check all appropriate)
☐ Jointed at neck ☐ Elbows ☐ Waist ☐ Wrist
☐ Hips ☐ Knees ☐ Ankles
☐ Other _____

Torso
    Material _____

Arms (check one)
☐ Ball jointed ☐ Bent limb ☐ Straight wrist
    Material _____

Legs (check one)
☐ Ball jointed ☐ Bent limb ☐ Straight
    Material _____

Mark(s) on Body
    Where located _____
    Stamped, incised: _____
    Signed by ☐ Artist ☐ Manufacturer

Clothing (check one)
☐ Original to doll ☐ Contemporary with doll

Replacement clothing made by _____
_____

Outerwear
    Style_____
    _____

    Fabric _____
    _____

    Color _____

    Trim_____

Underwear
    Fabric _____
    _____

    Trim _____

Accessories_____
_____
_____

References
References: (Book magazine article, internet)
    Source, author, page# _____
    _____
    _____

For a similar doll, see:_____
_____
_____

Ribbons & Awards: _____
_____
_____
_____

My Doll Organizer©

Doll # _____

Photo

Head Markings:

Body Markings:

Name of Doll _____

Maker of Doll _____

Height _____

Acquired from _____

    When acquired _____

    Purchase price $ _____

    Replacement cost (book value) $ _____

    Value (date & source) $ _____

    _____

Category/Type of doll _____

Condition _____

_____

_____

Repairs _____

_____

_____

_____

    Done by _____

    Repair date _____

    Repair cost _____

Original box, tags, other _____

_____

_____

Head

Material (check one)
- ☐ Bisque ☐ Celluloid ☐ China ☐ Cloth
- ☐ Composition ☐ Hard Plastic ☐ Papier-mâché
- ☐ Vinyl ☐ Wax ☐ Wood ☐ Other _____

Type (check one)
- ☐ Socket ☐ Flange ☐ Shoulder head
- ☐ Head on shoulder plate ☐ Other _____

Hair (check one)
- ☐ Wig (☐ Mohair ☐ Human Hair ☐ Synthetic
  ☐ Other _____)
- ☐ Molded Hair ☐ Painted ☐ Other _____
- Hair color _____

Eyes (check one)
- ☐ Glass (☐ Set ☐ Sleeping ☐ Flirty
  ☐ Paperweight ☐ Threaded)
- ☐ Decal ☐ Intaglio ☐ Metal ☐ Painted
- ☐ Eyelashes painted ☐ Hair eyelashes
- ☐ Synthetic lashes

Mouth (check one)
- ☐ Closed mouth ☐ Open/Closed ☐ Open mouth
- ☐ Teeth ☐ Tongue
- ☐ Other _____

Ears (check one)
- ☐ Pierced in head ☐ Pierced through lobe
- ☐ Applied ☐ Other _____

Body (check all appropriate)
- ☐ Jointed at neck ☐ Elbows ☐ Waist ☐ Wrist
- ☐ Hips ☐ Knees ☐ Ankles
- ☐ Other _____

Torso
  Material _____

Arms (check one)
- ☐ Ball jointed ☐ Bent limb ☐ Straight wrist
  Material _____

Legs (check one)
- ☐ Ball jointed ☐ Bent limb ☐ Straight
  Material _____

Mark(s) on Body
  Where located _____
  Stamped, incised: _____
  Signed by ☐ Artist ☐ Manufacturer

Clothing (check one)
- ☐ Original to doll ☐ Contemporary with doll

Replacement clothing made by _____
_____

Outerwear
  Style _____
  _____

  Fabric _____
  _____

  Color _____

  Trim _____

Underwear
  Fabric _____
  _____

  Trim _____

Accessories _____
_____
_____

References
References: (Book magazine article, internet)
  Source, author, page# _____
  _____
  _____

For a similar doll, see: _____
_____
_____

Ribbons & Awards: _____
_____
_____
_____

My Doll Organizer©

Doll # _____

Photo

Head Markings:

Body Markings:

Name of Doll _____

Maker of Doll _____

Height _____

Acquired from _____

    When acquired _____

    Purchase price $ _____

    Replacement cost (book value) $ _____

    Value (date & source) $ _____

_____

Category/Type of doll _____

Condition _____

_____

_____

Repairs _____

_____

_____

    Done by _____

    Repair date _____

    Repair cost _____

Original box, tags, other _____

_____

_____

Head

Material (check one)
- ☐ Bisque ☐ Celluloid ☐ China ☐ Cloth
- ☐ Composition ☐ Hard Plastic ☐ Papier-mâché
- ☐ Vinyl ☐ Wax ☐ Wood ☐ Other _____

Type (check one)
- ☐ Socket ☐ Flange ☐ Shoulder head
- ☐ Head on shoulder plate ☐ Other _____

Hair (check one)
- ☐ Wig (☐ Mohair ☐ Human Hair ☐ Synthetic
  - ☐ Other _____)
- ☐ Molded Hair ☐ Painted ☐ Other _____
- Hair color _____

Eyes (check one)
- ☐ Glass (☐ Set ☐ Sleeping ☐ Flirty
  - ☐ Paperweight ☐ Threaded)
- ☐ Decal ☐ Intaglio ☐ Metal ☐ Painted
- ☐ Eyelashes painted ☐ Hair eyelashes
- ☐ Synthetic lashes

Mouth (check one)
- ☐ Closed mouth ☐ Open/Closed ☐ Open mouth
- ☐ Teeth ☐ Tongue
- ☐ Other _____

Ears (check one)
- ☐ Pierced in head ☐ Pierced through lobe
- ☐ Applied ☐ Other _____

Body (check all appropriate)
- ☐ Jointed at neck ☐ Elbows ☐ Waist ☐ Wrist
- ☐ Hips ☐ Knees ☐ Ankles
- ☐ Other _____

Torso
- Material _____

Arms (check one)
- ☐ Ball jointed ☐ Bent limb ☐ Straight wrist
- Material _____

Legs (check one)
- ☐ Ball jointed ☐ Bent limb ☐ Straight
- Material _____

Mark(s) on Body
- Where located _____
- Stamped, incised: _____
- Signed by ☐ Artist ☐ Manufacturer

Clothing (check one)
- ☐ Original to doll ☐ Contemporary with doll

Replacement clothing made by _____
_____

Outerwear
- Style _____
_____
- Fabric _____
_____
- Color _____
- Trim _____

Underwear
- Fabric _____
_____
- Trim _____

Accessories _____
_____
_____

References
References: (Book magazine article, internet)
- Source, author, page# _____
_____
_____

For a similar doll, see: _____
_____
_____

Ribbons & Awards: _____
_____
_____
_____

My Doll Organizer©

Doll # _____

Photo

Head Markings:

Body Markings:

Name of Doll _____

Maker of Doll _____

Height _____

Acquired from _____

    When acquired _____

    Purchase price $ _____

    Replacement cost (book value) $ _____

    Value (date & source) $ _____

    _____

Category/Type of doll _____

Condition _____

_____

_____

Repairs _____

_____

_____

_____

    Done by _____

    Repair date _____

    Repair cost _____

Original box, tags, other _____

_____

_____

Head

Material (check one)
- [ ] Bisque [ ] Celluloid [ ] China [ ] Cloth
- [ ] Composition [ ] Hard Plastic [ ] Papier-mâché
- [ ] Vinyl [ ] Wax [ ] Wood [ ] Other _____

Type (check one)
- [ ] Socket [ ] Flange [ ] Shoulder head
- [ ] Head on shoulder plate [ ] Other _____

Hair (check one)
- [ ] Wig ([ ] Mohair [ ] Human Hair [ ] Synthetic
        [ ] Other_____)
- [ ] Molded Hair [ ] Painted [ ] Other _____
- Hair color _____

Eyes (check one)
- [ ] Glass ([ ] Set [ ] Sleeping [ ] Flirty
        [ ] Paperweight [ ] Threaded)
- [ ] Decal [ ] Intaglio [ ] Metal [ ] Painted
- [ ] Eyelashes painted [ ] Hair eyelashes
- [ ] Synthetic lashes

Mouth (check one)
- [ ] Closed mouth [ ] Open/Closed [ ] Open mouth
- [ ] Teeth [ ] Tongue
- [ ] Other _____

Ears (check one)
- [ ] Pierced in head [ ] Pierced through lobe
- [ ] Applied [ ] Other _____

Body (check all appropriate)
- [ ] Jointed at neck [ ] Elbows [ ] Waist [ ] Wrist
- [ ] Hips [ ] Knees [ ] Ankles
- [ ] Other _____

Torso
- Material _____

Arms (check one)
- [ ] Ball jointed [ ] Bent limb [ ] Straight wrist
- Material _____

Legs (check one)
- [ ] Ball jointed [ ] Bent limb [ ] Straight
- Material _____

Mark(s) on Body
- Where located _____
- Stamped, incised: _____
- Signed by [ ] Artist [ ] Manufacturer

Clothing (check one)
- [ ] Original to doll [ ] Contemporary with doll

Replacement clothing made by _____
_____

Outerwear
- Style_____
  _____
- Fabric _____
  _____
- Color _____
- Trim_____

Underwear
- Fabric _____
  _____
- Trim_____

Accessories_____
_____
_____

References
References: (Book magazine article, internet)
- Source, author, page# _____
  _____
  _____

For a similar doll, see:_____
_____
_____

Ribbons & Awards: _____
_____
_____
_____

My Doll Organizer©

Doll # _____

Photo

Head Markings:

Body Markings:

Name of Doll _____

Maker of Doll _____

Height _____

Acquired from _____

When acquired _____

Purchase price $_____

Replacement cost (book value) $_____

Value (date & source) $_____

_____

Category/Type of doll _____

Condition _____

_____

_____

Repairs _____

_____

_____

_____

Done by _____

Repair date _____

Repair cost _____

Original box, tags, other _____

_____

_____

Head

Material (check one)
- ☐ Bisque ☐ Celluloid ☐ China ☐ Cloth
- ☐ Composition ☐ Hard Plastic ☐ Papier-mâché
- ☐ Vinyl ☐ Wax ☐ Wood ☐ Other _____

Type (check one)
- ☐ Socket ☐ Flange ☐ Shoulder head
- ☐ Head on shoulder plate ☐ Other _____

Hair (check one)
- ☐ Wig (☐ Mohair ☐ Human Hair ☐ Synthetic
  - ☐ Other _____)
- ☐ Molded Hair ☐ Painted ☐ Other _____
- Hair color _____

Eyes (check one)
- ☐ Glass (☐ Set ☐ Sleeping ☐ Flirty
  - ☐ Paperweight ☐ Threaded)
- ☐ Decal ☐ Intaglio ☐ Metal ☐ Painted
- ☐ Eyelashes painted ☐ Hair eyelashes
- ☐ Synthetic lashes

Mouth (check one)
- ☐ Closed mouth ☐ Open/Closed ☐ Open mouth
- ☐ Teeth ☐ Tongue
- ☐ Other _____

Ears (check one)
- ☐ Pierced in head ☐ Pierced through lobe
- ☐ Applied ☐ Other _____

Body (check all appropriate)
- ☐ Jointed at neck ☐ Elbows ☐ Waist ☐ Wrist
- ☐ Hips ☐ Knees ☐ Ankles
- ☐ Other _____

Torso
- Material _____

Arms (check one)
- ☐ Ball jointed ☐ Bent limb ☐ Straight wrist
- Material _____

Legs (check one)
- ☐ Ball jointed ☐ Bent limb ☐ Straight
- Material _____

Mark(s) on Body
- Where located _____
- Stamped, incised: _____
- Signed by ☐ Artist ☐ Manufacturer

Clothing (check one)
- ☐ Original to doll ☐ Contemporary with doll

Replacement clothing made by _____
_____

Outerwear
- Style _____
  _____
- Fabric _____
  _____
- Color _____
- Trim _____

Underwear
- Fabric _____
  _____
- Trim _____

Accessories _____
_____
_____

References
References: (Book magazine article, internet)
- Source, author, page# _____
  _____
  _____

For a similar doll, see: _____
_____
_____

Ribbons & Awards: _____
_____
_____
_____
_____

My Doll Organizer©

Doll # _____

Photo

Head Markings:

Body Markings:

Name of Doll _____

Maker of Doll _____

Height _____

Acquired from _____

    When acquired _____

    Purchase price $ _____

    Replacement cost (book value) $_____

    Value (date & source) $_____

                        _____

Category/Type of doll _____

Condition _____

_____

_____

Repairs _____

_____

_____

_____

    Done by _____

    Repair date _____

    Repair cost _____

Original box, tags, other _____

_____

_____

Head

Material (check one)
- ☐ Bisque ☐ Celluloid ☐ China ☐ Cloth
- ☐ Composition ☐ Hard Plastic ☐ Papier-mâché
- ☐ Vinyl ☐ Wax ☐ Wood ☐ Other _____

Type (check one)
- ☐ Socket ☐ Flange ☐ Shoulder head
- ☐ Head on shoulder plate ☐ Other _____

Hair (check one)
- ☐ Wig (☐ Mohair ☐ Human Hair ☐ Synthetic
  - ☐ Other _____)
- ☐ Molded Hair ☐ Painted ☐ Other _____
- Hair color _____

Eyes (check one)
- ☐ Glass (☐ Set ☐ Sleeping ☐ Flirty
  - ☐ Paperweight ☐ Threaded)
- ☐ Decal ☐ Intaglio ☐ Metal ☐ Painted
- ☐ Eyelashes painted ☐ Hair eyelashes
- ☐ Synthetic lashes

Mouth (check one)
- ☐ Closed mouth ☐ Open/Closed ☐ Open mouth
- ☐ Teeth ☐ Tongue
- ☐ Other _____

Ears (check one)
- ☐ Pierced in head ☐ Pierced through lobe
- ☐ Applied ☐ Other _____

Body (check all appropriate)
- ☐ Jointed at neck ☐ Elbows ☐ Waist ☐ Wrist
- ☐ Hips ☐ Knees ☐ Ankles
- ☐ Other _____

Torso
- Material _____

Arms (check one)
- ☐ Ball jointed ☐ Bent limb ☐ Straight wrist
- Material _____

Legs (check one)
- ☐ Ball jointed ☐ Bent limb ☐ Straight
- Material _____

Mark(s) on Body
- Where located _____
- Stamped, incised: _____
- Signed by ☐ Artist ☐ Manufacturer

Clothing (check one)
- ☐ Original to doll ☐ Contemporary with doll

Replacement clothing made by _____
_____

Outerwear
- Style _____
  - _____
- Fabric _____
  - _____
- Color _____
- Trim _____

Underwear
- Fabric _____
  - _____
- Trim _____

Accessories _____
_____
_____

References
References: (Book magazine article, internet)
- Source, author, page# _____
  - _____
  - _____

For a similar doll, see: _____
_____
_____
_____

Ribbons & Awards: _____
_____
_____
_____

My Doll Organizer©

My Doll Organizer

Doll # _____

Photo

Head Markings:

Body Markings:

Name of Doll _____

Maker of Doll _____

Height _____

Acquired from _____

When acquired _____

Purchase price $_____

Replacement cost (book value) $_____

Value (date & source) $_____

_____

Category/Type of doll _____

Condition _____

Repairs _____

_____

_____

_____

Done by _____

Repair date _____

Repair cost _____

Original box, tags, other _____

_____

_____

Head

Material (check one)
☐ Bisque ☐ Celluloid ☐ China ☐ Cloth
☐ Composition ☐ Hard Plastic ☐ Papier-mâché
☐ Vinyl ☐ Wax ☐ Wood ☐ Other _____

Type (check one)
☐ Socket ☐ Flange ☐ Shoulder head
☐ Head on shoulder plate ☐ Other _____

Hair (check one)
☐ Wig (☐ Mohair ☐ Human Hair ☐ Synthetic
　　☐ Other_____)
☐ Molded Hair ☐ Painted ☐ Other _____
Hair color _____

Eyes (check one)
☐ Glass (☐ Set ☐ Sleeping ☐ Flirty
　　☐ Paperweight ☐ Threaded)
☐ Decal ☐ Intaglio ☐ Metal ☐ Painted
☐ Eyelashes painted ☐ Hair eyelashes
☐ Synthetic lashes

Mouth (check one)
☐ Closed mouth ☐ Open/Closed ☐ Open mouth
☐ Teeth ☐ Tongue
☐ Other _____

Ears (check one)
☐ Pierced in head ☐ Pierced through lobe
☐ Applied ☐ Other _____

Body (check all appropriate)
☐ Jointed at neck ☐ Elbows ☐ Waist ☐ Wrist
☐ Hips ☐ Knees ☐ Ankles
☐ Other _____

Torso
　Material _____

Arms (check one)
☐ Ball jointed ☐ Bent limb ☐ Straight wrist
　Material _____

Legs (check one)
☐ Ball jointed ☐ Bent limb ☐ Straight
　Material _____

Mark(s) on Body
　Where located _____
　Stamped, incised: _____
　Signed by ☐ Artist ☐ Manufacturer

Clothing (check one)
☐ Original to doll ☐ Contemporary with doll

Replacement clothing made by _____
_____

Outerwear
　Style_____
　_____
　Fabric _____
　_____
　Color _____
　Trim_____

Underwear
　Fabric _____
　_____
　Trim_____

Accessories_____
_____
_____

References
References: (Book magazine article, internet)
　Source, author, page# _____
　_____
　_____
　_____

For a similar doll, see:_____
_____
_____

Ribbons & Awards: _____
_____
_____
_____

My Doll Organizer©

Doll # _____

Photo

Head Markings:

Body Markings:

Name of Doll _____

Maker of Doll _____

Height _____

Acquired from _____

    When acquired _____

    Purchase price $ _____

    Replacement cost (book value) $ _____

    Value (date & source) $ _____

    _____

Category/Type of doll _____

Condition _____

_____

Repairs _____

_____

_____

_____

    Done by _____

    Repair date _____

    Repair cost _____

Original box, tags, other _____

_____

_____

Head

Material (check one)
☐ Bisque ☐ Celluloid ☐ China ☐ Cloth
☐ Composition ☐ Hard Plastic ☐ Papier-mâché
☐ Vinyl ☐ Wax ☐ Wood ☐ Other_____

Type (check one)
☐ Socket ☐ Flange ☐ Shoulder head
☐ Head on shoulder plate ☐ Other_____

Hair (check one)
☐ Wig (☐ Mohair ☐ Human Hair ☐ Synthetic
☐ Other_____)
☐ Molded Hair ☐ Painted ☐ Other _____
Hair color _____

Eyes (check one)
☐ Glass (☐ Set ☐ Sleeping ☐ Flirty
☐ Paperweight ☐ Threaded)
☐ Decal ☐ Intaglio ☐ Metal ☐ Painted
☐ Eyelashes painted ☐ Hair eyelashes
☐ Synthetic lashes

Mouth (check one)
☐ Closed mouth ☐ Open/Closed ☐ Open mouth
☐ Teeth ☐ Tongue
☐ Other _____

Ears (check one)
☐ Pierced in head ☐ Pierced through lobe
☐ Applied ☐ Other _____

Body (check all appropriate)
☐ Jointed at neck ☐ Elbows ☐ Waist ☐ Wrist
☐ Hips ☐ Knees ☐ Ankles
☐ Other _____

Torso
Material _____

Arms (check one)
☐ Ball jointed ☐ Bent limb ☐ Straight wrist
Material _____

Legs (check one)
☐ Ball jointed ☐ Bent limb ☐ Straight
Material _____

Mark(s) on Body
Where located _____
Stamped, incised: _____
Signed by ☐ Artist ☐ Manufacturer

Clothing (check one)
☐ Original to doll ☐ Contemporary with doll

Replacement clothing made by _____
_____

Outerwear
Style_____
_____

Fabric _____
_____

Color _____

Trim_____

Underwear
Fabric _____
_____

Trim_____

Accessories_____
_____

References
References: (Book magazine article, internet)
Source, author, page# _____
_____
_____

For a similar doll, see:_____
_____
_____

Ribbons & Awards: _____
_____
_____
_____

My Doll Organizer©

My Doll Organizer©

Doll # _____

Photo

Head Markings:

Body Markings:

Name of Doll _____

Maker of Doll _____

Height _____

Acquired from _____

When acquired _____

Purchase price $ _____

Replacement cost (book value) $ _____

Value (date & source) $ _____

_____

Category/Type of doll _____

Condition _____

_____

_____

Repairs _____

_____

_____

_____

Done by _____

Repair date _____

Repair cost _____

Original box, tags, other _____

_____

_____

Head

Material (check one)

☐ Bisque ☐ Celluloid ☐ China ☐ Cloth
☐ Composition ☐ Hard Plastic ☐ Papier-mâché
☐ Vinyl ☐ Wax ☐ Wood ☐ Other_____

Type (check one)

☐ Socket ☐ Flange ☐ Shoulder head
☐ Head on shoulder plate ☐ Other_____

Hair (check one)

☐ Wig (☐ Mohair ☐ Human Hair ☐ Synthetic
☐ Other_____)
☐ Molded Hair ☐ Painted ☐ Other_____
Hair color_____

Eyes (check one)

☐ Glass (☐ Set ☐ Sleeping ☐ Flirty
☐ Paperweight ☐ Threaded)
☐ Decal ☐ Intaglio ☐ Metal ☐ Painted
☐ Eyelashes painted ☐ Hair eyelashes
☐ Synthetic lashes

Mouth (check one)

☐ Closed mouth ☐ Open/Closed ☐ Open mouth
☐ Teeth ☐ Tongue
☐ Other_____

Ears (check one)

☐ Pierced in head ☐ Pierced through lobe
☐ Applied ☐ Other_____

Body (check all appropriate)

☐ Jointed at neck ☐ Elbows ☐ Waist ☐ Wrist
☐ Hips ☐ Knees ☐ Ankles
☐ Other_____

Torso

Material_____

Arms (check one)

☐ Ball jointed ☐ Bent limb ☐ Straight wrist
Material_____

Legs (check one)

☐ Ball jointed ☐ Bent limb ☐ Straight
Material_____

Mark(s) on Body

Where located_____
Stamped, incised:_____
Signed by ☐ Artist ☐ Manufacturer

Clothing (check one)

☐ Original to doll ☐ Contemporary with doll

Replacement clothing made by_____
_____

Outerwear

Style_____
_____

Fabric_____
_____

Color_____

Trim_____

Underwear

Fabric_____
_____

Trim_____

Accessories_____
_____

References

References: (Book magazine article, internet)

Source, author, page#_____
_____
_____

For a similar doll, see:_____
_____
_____

Ribbons & Awards:_____
_____
_____
_____

My Doll Organizer©

Doll # _____

Photo

Head Markings:

Body Markings:

Name of Doll _____

Maker of Doll _____

Height _____

Acquired from _____

    When acquired _____

    Purchase price $_____

    Replacement cost (book value) $_____

    Value (date & source) $_____

                 _____

Category/Type of doll _____

Condition _____

_____

Repairs _____

_____

_____

_____

    Done by _____

    Repair date _____

    Repair cost _____

Original box, tags, other _____

_____

_____

Head

Material (check one)
☐ Bisque ☐ Celluloid ☐ China ☐ Cloth
☐ Composition ☐ Hard Plastic ☐ Papier-mâché
☐ Vinyl ☐ Wax ☐ Wood ☐ Other _____

Type (check one)
☐ Socket ☐ Flange ☐ Shoulder head
☐ Head on shoulder plate ☐ Other _____

Hair (check one)
☐ Wig (☐ Mohair ☐ Human Hair ☐ Synthetic
　　　☐ Other_____)
☐ Molded Hair ☐ Painted ☐ Other _____
Hair color _____

Eyes (check one)
☐ Glass (☐ Set ☐ Sleeping ☐ Flirty
　　　☐ Paperweight ☐ Threaded)
☐ Decal ☐ Intaglio ☐ Metal ☐ Painted
☐ Eyelashes painted ☐ Hair eyelashes
☐ Synthetic lashes

Mouth (check one)
☐ Closed mouth ☐ Open/Closed ☐ Open mouth
☐ Teeth ☐ Tongue
☐ Other _____

Ears (check one)
☐ Pierced in head ☐ Pierced through lobe
☐ Applied ☐ Other _____

Body (check all appropriate)
☐ Jointed at neck ☐ Elbows ☐ Waist ☐ Wrist
☐ Hips ☐ Knees ☐ Ankles
☐ Other _____

Torso
Material _____

Arms (check one)
☐ Ball jointed ☐ Bent limb ☐ Straight wrist
Material _____

Legs (check one)
☐ Ball jointed ☐ Bent limb ☐ Straight
Material _____

Mark(s) on Body
Where located _____
Stamped, incised: _____
Signed by ☐ Artist ☐ Manufacturer

Clothing (check one)
☐ Original to doll ☐ Contemporary with doll

Replacement clothing made by _____
_____

Outerwear
Style_____
　　　_____

Fabric _____
　　　_____

Color _____

Trim_____

Underwear
Fabric _____
　　　_____

Trim_____

Accessories_____
_____
_____

References
References: (Book magazine article, internet)
Source, author, page# _____
_____
_____

For a similar doll, see:_____
_____
_____

Ribbons & Awards: _____
_____
_____
_____

My Doll Organizer©

My Doll Organizer©

Doll # _____

Photo

Head Markings:

Body Markings:

Name of Doll _____

Maker of Doll _____

Height _____

Acquired from _____

    When acquired _____

    Purchase price $_____

    Replacement cost (book value) $_____

    Value (date & source) $_____

    _____

Category/Type of doll _____

Condition _____

_____

_____

Repairs _____

_____

_____

_____

    Done by _____

    Repair date _____

    Repair cost _____

Original box, tags, other _____

_____

_____

Head

Material (check one)

☐ Bisque ☐ Celluloid ☐ China ☐ Cloth
☐ Composition ☐ Hard Plastic ☐ Papier-mâché
☐ Vinyl ☐ Wax ☐ Wood ☐ Other _____

Type (check one)

☐ Socket ☐ Flange ☐ Shoulder head
☐ Head on shoulder plate ☐ Other _____

Hair (check one)

☐ Wig (☐ Mohair ☐ Human Hair ☐ Synthetic
     ☐ Other_____)
☐ Molded Hair ☐ Painted ☐ Other _____
Hair color _____

Eyes (check one)

☐ Glass (☐ Set ☐ Sleeping ☐ Flirty
     ☐ Paperweight ☐ Threaded)
☐ Decal ☐ Intaglio ☐ Metal ☐ Painted
☐ Eyelashes painted ☐ Hair eyelashes
☐ Synthetic lashes

Mouth (check one)

☐ Closed mouth ☐ Open/Closed ☐ Open mouth
☐ Teeth ☐ Tongue
☐ Other _____

Ears (check one)

☐ Pierced in head ☐ Pierced through lobe
☐ Applied ☐ Other _____

Body (check all appropriate)

☐ Jointed at neck ☐ Elbows ☐ Waist ☐ Wrist
☐ Hips ☐ Knees ☐ Ankles
☐ Other _____

Torso

Material _____

Arms (check one)

☐ Ball jointed ☐ Bent limb ☐ Straight wrist
Material _____

Legs (check one)

☐ Ball jointed ☐ Bent limb ☐ Straight
Material _____

Mark(s) on Body

Where located _____
Stamped, incised: _____
Signed by ☐ Artist ☐ Manufacturer

Clothing (check one)

☐ Original to doll ☐ Contemporary with doll

Replacement clothing made by _____
_____

Outerwear

  Style_____
     _____

  Fabric _____
     _____

  Color _____

  Trim_____

Underwear

  Fabric _____
     _____

  Trim_____

Accessories_____
_____
_____

References

References: (Book magazine article, internet)
  Source, author, page# _____
  _____
  _____

For a similar doll, see:_____
_____
_____

Ribbons & Awards: _____
_____
_____
_____

My Doll Organizer©

Doll # _____

Photo

Head Markings:

Body Markings:

Name of Doll _____

Maker of Doll _____

Height _____

Acquired from _____

    When acquired _____

    Purchase price $_____

    Replacement cost (book value) $_____

    Value (date & source) $_____

    _____

Category/Type of doll _____

Condition _____

_____

_____

Repairs _____

_____

_____

_____

    Done by _____

    Repair date _____

    Repair cost _____

Original box, tags, other _____

_____

_____

Head

Material (check one)
☐ Bisque ☐ Celluloid ☐ China ☐ Cloth
☐ Composition ☐ Hard Plastic ☐ Papier-mâché
☐ Vinyl ☐ Wax ☐ Wood ☐ Other _____

Type (check one)
☐ Socket ☐ Flange ☐ Shoulder head
☐ Head on shoulder plate ☐ Other _____

Hair (check one)
☐ Wig (☐ Mohair ☐ Human Hair ☐ Synthetic
☐ Other_____)
☐ Molded Hair ☐ Painted ☐ Other _____
Hair color _____

Eyes (check one)
☐ Glass (☐ Set ☐ Sleeping ☐ Flirty
☐ Paperweight ☐ Threaded)
☐ Decal ☐ Intaglio ☐ Metal ☐ Painted
☐ Eyelashes painted ☐ Hair eyelashes
☐ Synthetic lashes

Mouth (check one)
☐ Closed mouth ☐ Open/Closed ☐ Open mouth
☐ Teeth ☐ Tongue
☐ Other _____

Ears (check one)
☐ Pierced in head ☐ Pierced through lobe
☐ Applied ☐ Other _____

Body (check all appropriate)
☐ Jointed at neck ☐ Elbows ☐ Waist ☐ Wrist
☐ Hips ☐ Knees ☐ Ankles
☐ Other _____

Torso
Material _____

Arms (check one)
☐ Ball jointed ☐ Bent limb ☐ Straight wrist
Material _____

Legs (check one)
☐ Ball jointed ☐ Bent limb ☐ Straight
Material _____

Mark(s) on Body
Where located _____
Stamped, incised: _____
Signed by ☐ Artist ☐ Manufacturer

Clothing (check one)
☐ Original to doll ☐ Contemporary with doll

Replacement clothing made by _____
_____

Outerwear
Style_____
_____

Fabric _____
_____

Color _____

Trim_____

Underwear
Fabric _____
_____

Trim_____

Accessories_____
_____
_____

References
References: (Book magazine article, internet)
Source, author, page# _____
_____
_____

For a similar doll, see:_____
_____
_____

Ribbons & Awards: _____
_____
_____
_____

My Doll Organizer©

Doll # _____

Photo

Head Markings:

Body Markings:

Name of Doll _____

Maker of Doll _____

Height _____

Acquired from _____

    When acquired _____

    Purchase price $ _____

    Replacement cost (book value) $_____

    Value (date & source) $_____

    _____

Category/Type of doll _____

Condition _____

_____

Repairs _____

_____

_____

    Done by _____

    Repair date _____

    Repair cost _____

Original box, tags, other _____

_____

Head

Material (check one)
☐ Bisque ☐ Celluloid ☐ China ☐ Cloth
☐ Composition ☐ Hard Plastic ☐ Papier-mâché
☐ Vinyl ☐ Wax ☐ Wood ☐ Other _____

Type (check one)
☐ Socket ☐ Flange ☐ Shoulder head
☐ Head on shoulder plate ☐ Other _____

Hair (check one)
☐ Wig (☐ Mohair ☐ Human Hair ☐ Synthetic
　　　☐ Other _____)
☐ Molded Hair ☐ Painted ☐ Other _____
Hair color _____

Eyes (check one)
☐ Glass (☐ Set ☐ Sleeping ☐ Flirty
　　　☐ Paperweight ☐ Threaded)
☐ Decal ☐ Intaglio ☐ Metal ☐ Painted
☐ Eyelashes painted ☐ Hair eyelashes
☐ Synthetic lashes

Mouth (check one)
☐ Closed mouth ☐ Open/Closed ☐ Open mouth
☐ Teeth ☐ Tongue
☐ Other _____

Ears (check one)
☐ Pierced in head ☐ Pierced through lobe
☐ Applied ☐ Other _____

Body (check all appropriate)
☐ Jointed at neck ☐ Elbows ☐ Waist ☐ Wrist
☐ Hips ☐ Knees ☐ Ankles
☐ Other _____

Torso
Material _____

Arms (check one)
☐ Ball jointed ☐ Bent limb ☐ Straight wrist
Material _____

Legs (check one)
☐ Ball jointed ☐ Bent limb ☐ Straight
Material _____

Mark(s) on Body
Where located _____
Stamped, incised: _____
Signed by ☐ Artist ☐ Manufacturer

Clothing (check one)
☐ Original to doll ☐ Contemporary with doll

Replacement clothing made by _____
_____

Outerwear
Style _____
_____

Fabric _____
_____

Color _____

Trim _____

Underwear
Fabric _____
_____

Trim _____

Accessories _____
_____

References
References: (Book magazine article, internet)
Source, author, page# _____
_____
_____

For a similar doll, see: _____
_____
_____

Ribbons & Awards: _____
_____
_____

My Doll Organizer©

Doll # _____

Photo

Head Markings:

Body Markings:

Name of Doll _____

Maker of Doll _____

Height _____

Acquired from _____

When acquired _____

Purchase price $ _____

Replacement cost (book value) $ _____

Value (date & source) $ _____

_____

Category/Type of doll _____

Condition _____

Repairs _____

_____

_____

Done by _____

Repair date _____

Repair cost _____

Original box, tags, other _____

_____

_____

Head

Material (check one)
- ☐ Bisque ☐ Celluloid ☐ China ☐ Cloth
- ☐ Composition ☐ Hard Plastic ☐ Papier-mâché
- ☐ Vinyl ☐ Wax ☐ Wood ☐ Other _____

Type (check one)
- ☐ Socket ☐ Flange ☐ Shoulder head
- ☐ Head on shoulder plate ☐ Other _____

Hair (check one)
- ☐ Wig (☐ Mohair ☐ Human Hair ☐ Synthetic
  - ☐ Other_____)
- ☐ Molded Hair ☐ Painted ☐ Other _____
- Hair color _____

Eyes (check one)
- ☐ Glass (☐ Set ☐ Sleeping ☐ Flirty
  - ☐ Paperweight ☐ Threaded)
- ☐ Decal ☐ Intaglio ☐ Metal ☐ Painted
- ☐ Eyelashes painted ☐ Hair eyelashes
- ☐ Synthetic lashes

Mouth (check one)
- ☐ Closed mouth ☐ Open/Closed ☐ Open mouth
- ☐ Teeth ☐ Tongue
- ☐ Other _____

Ears (check one)
- ☐ Pierced in head ☐ Pierced through lobe
- ☐ Applied ☐ Other _____

Body (check all appropriate)
- ☐ Jointed at neck ☐ Elbows ☐ Waist ☐ Wrist
- ☐ Hips ☐ Knees ☐ Ankles
- ☐ Other _____

Torso
- Material _____

Arms (check one)
- ☐ Ball jointed ☐ Bent limb ☐ Straight wrist
- Material _____

Legs (check one)
- ☐ Ball jointed ☐ Bent limb ☐ Straight
- Material _____

Mark(s) on Body
- Where located _____
- Stamped, incised: _____
- Signed by ☐ Artist ☐ Manufacturer

Clothing (check one)
☐ Original to doll ☐ Contemporary with doll

Replacement clothing made by _____
_____

Outerwear
- Style_____
- _____
- Fabric _____
- _____
- Color _____
- Trim_____

Underwear
- Fabric _____
- _____
- Trim _____

Accessories_____
_____
_____

References
References: (Book magazine article, internet)
- Source, author, page# _____
- _____
- _____

For a similar doll, see:_____
_____
_____

Ribbons & Awards: _____
_____
_____
_____

My Doll Organizer©

Doll # _____

Photo

Head Markings:

Body Markings:

Name of Doll _____

Maker of Doll _____

Height _____

Acquired from _____

    When acquired _____

    Purchase price $ _____

    Replacement cost (book value) $ _____

    Value (date & source) $ _____

    _____

Category/Type of doll _____

Condition _____

_____

Repairs _____

_____

_____

    Done by _____

    Repair date _____

    Repair cost _____

Original box, tags, other _____

_____

Head

Material (check one)
□ Bisque □ Celluloid □ China □ Cloth
□ Composition □ Hard Plastic □ Papier-mâché
□ Vinyl □ Wax □ Wood □ Other_____

Type (check one)
□ Socket □ Flange □ Shoulder head
□ Head on shoulder plate □ Other_____

Hair (check one)
□ Wig (□ Mohair □ Human Hair □ Synthetic
        □ Other_____)
□ Molded Hair □ Painted □ Other _____
Hair color _____

Eyes (check one)
□ Glass (□ Set □ Sleeping □ Flirty
          □ Paperweight □ Threaded)
□ Decal □ Intaglio □ Metal □ Painted
□ Eyelashes painted □ Hair eyelashes
□ Synthetic lashes

Mouth (check one)
□ Closed mouth □ Open/Closed □ Open mouth
□ Teeth □ Tongue
□ Other _____

Ears (check one)
□ Pierced in head □ Pierced through lobe
□ Applied □ Other _____

Body (check all appropriate)
□ Jointed at neck □ Elbows □ Waist □ Wrist
□ Hips □ Knees □ Ankles
□ Other _____

Torso
Material _____

Arms (check one)
□ Ball jointed □ Bent limb □ Straight wrist
Material _____

Legs (check one)
□ Ball jointed □ Bent limb □ Straight
Material _____

Mark(s) on Body
Where located _____
Stamped, incised: _____
Signed by □ Artist □ Manufacturer

Clothing (check one)
□ Original to doll □ Contemporary with doll

Replacement clothing made by_____
_____

Outerwear
Style_____
_____

Fabric _____
_____

Color _____

Trim_____

Underwear
Fabric _____
_____

Trim_____

Accessories_____
_____

References
References: (Book magazine article, internet)
Source, author, page# _____
_____
_____

For a similar doll, see:_____
_____
_____

Ribbons & Awards: _____
_____
_____
_____
_____

My Doll Organizer[©]

Doll # _____

Photo

Head Markings:

Body Markings:

Name of Doll _____

Maker of Doll _____

Height _____

Acquired from _____

    When acquired _____

    Purchase price $ _____

    Replacement cost (book value) $ _____

    Value (date & source) $ _____

    _____

Category/Type of doll _____

Condition _____

_____

Repairs _____

_____

_____

    Done by _____

    Repair date _____

    Repair cost _____

Original box, tags, other _____

_____

Head

Material (check one)
- ☐ Bisque ☐ Celluloid ☐ China ☐ Cloth
- ☐ Composition ☐ Hard Plastic ☐ Papier-mâché
- ☐ Vinyl ☐ Wax ☐ Wood ☐ Other_____

Type (check one)
- ☐ Socket ☐ Flange ☐ Shoulder head
- ☐ Head on shoulder plate ☐ Other_____

Hair (check one)
- ☐ Wig (☐ Mohair ☐ Human Hair ☐ Synthetic
      ☐ Other_____)
- ☐ Molded Hair ☐ Painted ☐ Other_____
- Hair color _____

Eyes (check one)
- ☐ Glass (☐ Set ☐ Sleeping ☐ Flirty
      ☐ Paperweight ☐ Threaded)
- ☐ Decal ☐ Intaglio ☐ Metal ☐ Painted
- ☐ Eyelashes painted ☐ Hair eyelashes
- ☐ Synthetic lashes

Mouth (check one)
- ☐ Closed mouth ☐ Open/Closed ☐ Open mouth
- ☐ Teeth ☐ Tongue
- ☐ Other _____

Ears (check one)
- ☐ Pierced in head ☐ Pierced through lobe
- ☐ Applied ☐ Other _____

Body (check all appropriate)
- ☐ Jointed at neck ☐ Elbows ☐ Waist ☐ Wrist
- ☐ Hips ☐ Knees ☐ Ankles
- ☐ Other _____

Torso
- Material _____

Arms (check one)
- ☐ Ball jointed ☐ Bent limb ☐ Straight wrist
- Material _____

Legs (check one)
- ☐ Ball jointed ☐ Bent limb ☐ Straight
- Material _____

Mark(s) on Body
- Where located _____
- Stamped, incised: _____
- Signed by ☐ Artist ☐ Manufacturer

Clothing (check one)
- ☐ Original to doll ☐ Contemporary with doll

Replacement clothing made by _____
_____

Outerwear
- Style_____
  _____

- Fabric _____
  _____

- Color _____

- Trim_____

Underwear
- Fabric _____
  _____

- Trim _____

Accessories_____
_____
_____

References
References: (Book magazine article, internet)
- Source, author, page# _____
  _____
  _____

For a similar doll, see:_____
_____
_____

Ribbons & Awards: _____
_____
_____
_____

My Doll Organizer ©

Doll # _____

Tear carefully along perforation to remove.

Photo

Head Markings:

Body Markings:

Name of Doll _____

Maker of Doll _____

Height _____

Acquired from _____

    When acquired _____

    Purchase price $ _____

    Replacement cost (book value) $_____

    Value (date & source) $_____

    _____

Category/Type of doll _____

Condition _____

_____

Repairs _____

_____

_____

_____

    Done by _____

    Repair date _____

    Repair cost _____

Original box, tags, other _____

_____

_____

Head

Material (check one)
- ☐ Bisque ☐ Celluloid ☐ China ☐ Cloth
- ☐ Composition ☐ Hard Plastic ☐ Papier-mâché
- ☐ Vinyl ☐ Wax ☐ Wood ☐ Other _____

Type (check one)
- ☐ Socket ☐ Flange ☐ Shoulder head
- ☐ Head on shoulder plate ☐ Other _____

Hair (check one)
- ☐ Wig (☐ Mohair ☐ Human Hair ☐ Synthetic
  - ☐ Other_____)
- ☐ Molded Hair ☐ Painted ☐ Other _____
- Hair color _____

Eyes (check one)
- ☐ Glass (☐ Set ☐ Sleeping ☐ Flirty
  - ☐ Paperweight ☐ Threaded)
- ☐ Decal ☐ Intaglio ☐ Metal ☐ Painted
- ☐ Eyelashes painted ☐ Hair eyelashes
- ☐ Synthetic lashes

Mouth (check one)
- ☐ Closed mouth ☐ Open/Closed ☐ Open mouth
- ☐ Teeth ☐ Tongue
- ☐ Other _____

Ears (check one)
- ☐ Pierced in head ☐ Pierced through lobe
- ☐ Applied ☐ Other _____

Body (check all appropriate)
- ☐ Jointed at neck ☐ Elbows ☐ Waist ☐ Wrist
- ☐ Hips ☐ Knees ☐ Ankles
- ☐ Other _____

Torso
- Material _____

Arms (check one)
- ☐ Ball jointed ☐ Bent limb ☐ Straight wrist
- Material _____

Legs (check one)
- ☐ Ball jointed ☐ Bent limb ☐ Straight
- Material _____

Mark(s) on Body
- Where located _____
- Stamped, incised: _____
- Signed by ☐ Artist ☐ Manufacturer

Clothing (check one)
- ☐ Original to doll ☐ Contemporary with doll

Replacement clothing made by _____
_____

Outerwear
- Style_____
- _____
- Fabric _____
- _____
- Color _____
- Trim_____

Underwear
- Fabric _____
- _____
- Trim_____

Accessories_____
_____

References
References: (Book magazine article, internet)
- Source, author, page# _____
- _____
- _____

For a similar doll, see: _____
_____
_____

Ribbons & Awards: _____
_____
_____
_____

My Doll Organizer©

Doll # _____

Photo

Head Markings:

Body Markings:

Name of Doll _____

Maker of Doll _____

Height _____

Acquired from _____

   When acquired _____

   Purchase price $ _____

   Replacement cost (book value) $ _____

   Value (date & source) $ _____

   _____

Category/Type of doll _____

Condition _____

_____

_____

Repairs _____

_____

_____

_____

   Done by _____

   Repair date _____

   Repair cost _____

Original box, tags, other _____

_____

_____

Head

Material (check one)
- ☐ Bisque ☐ Celluloid ☐ China ☐ Cloth
- ☐ Composition ☐ Hard Plastic ☐ Papier-mâché
- ☐ Vinyl ☐ Wax ☐ Wood ☐ Other_____

Type (check one)
- ☐ Socket ☐ Flange ☐ Shoulder head
- ☐ Head on shoulder plate ☐ Other_____

Hair (check one)
- ☐ Wig (☐ Mohair ☐ Human Hair ☐ Synthetic
      ☐ Other_____)
- ☐ Molded Hair ☐ Painted ☐ Other_____
- Hair color _____

Eyes (check one)
- ☐ Glass (☐ Set ☐ Sleeping ☐ Flirty
      ☐ Paperweight ☐ Threaded)
- ☐ Decal ☐ Intaglio ☐ Metal ☐ Painted
- ☐ Eyelashes painted ☐ Hair eyelashes
- ☐ Synthetic lashes

Mouth (check one)
- ☐ Closed mouth ☐ Open/Closed ☐ Open mouth
- ☐ Teeth ☐ Tongue
- ☐ Other _____

Ears (check one)
- ☐ Pierced in head ☐ Pierced through lobe
- ☐ Applied ☐ Other _____

Body (check all appropriate)
- ☐ Jointed at neck ☐ Elbows ☐ Waist ☐ Wrist
- ☐ Hips ☐ Knees ☐ Ankles
- ☐ Other _____

Torso
- Material _____

Arms (check one)
- ☐ Ball jointed ☐ Bent limb ☐ Straight wrist
- Material _____

Legs (check one)
- ☐ Ball jointed ☐ Bent limb ☐ Straight
- Material _____

Mark(s) on Body
- Where located _____
- Stamped, incised: _____
- Signed by ☐ Artist ☐ Manufacturer

Clothing (check one)
- ☐ Original to doll ☐ Contemporary with doll

Replacement clothing made by_____
_____

Outerwear
- Style_____
  _____

- Fabric_____
  _____

- Color_____

- Trim_____

Underwear
- Fabric_____
  _____

- Trim_____

Accessories_____
_____
_____

References
References: (Book magazine article, internet)
- Source, author, page# _____
  _____
  _____

For a similar doll, see:_____
_____
_____

Ribbons & Awards: _____
_____
_____
_____

My Doll Organizer©

Doll # _____

Photo

Head Markings:

Body Markings:

Name of Doll _____

Maker of Doll _____

Height _____

Acquired from _____

    When acquired _____

    Purchase price $_____

    Replacement cost (book value) $_____

    Value (date & source) $_____

    _____

Category/Type of doll _____

Condition _____

_____

Repairs _____

_____

_____

_____

    Done by _____

    Repair date _____

    Repair cost _____

Original box, tags, other _____

_____

_____

_____

Head

Material (check one)
- ☐ Bisque ☐ Celluloid ☐ China ☐ Cloth
- ☐ Composition ☐ Hard Plastic ☐ Papier-mâché
- ☐ Vinyl ☐ Wax ☐ Wood ☐ Other_____

Type (check one)
- ☐ Socket ☐ Flange ☐ Shoulder head
- ☐ Head on shoulder plate ☐ Other_____

Hair (check one)
- ☐ Wig (☐ Mohair ☐ Human Hair ☐ Synthetic
      ☐ Other_____)
- ☐ Molded Hair ☐ Painted ☐ Other_____
- Hair color_____

Eyes (check one)
- ☐ Glass (☐ Set ☐ Sleeping ☐ Flirty
      ☐ Paperweight ☐ Threaded)
- ☐ Decal ☐ Intaglio ☐ Metal ☐ Painted
- ☐ Eyelashes painted ☐ Hair eyelashes
- ☐ Synthetic lashes

Mouth (check one)
- ☐ Closed mouth ☐ Open/Closed ☐ Open mouth
- ☐ Teeth ☐ Tongue
- ☐ Other_____

Ears (check one)
- ☐ Pierced in head ☐ Pierced through lobe
- ☐ Applied ☐ Other_____

Body (check all appropriate)
- ☐ Jointed at neck ☐ Elbows ☐ Waist ☐ Wrist
- ☐ Hips ☐ Knees ☐ Ankles
- ☐ Other_____

Torso
- Material_____

Arms (check one)
- ☐ Ball jointed ☐ Bent limb ☐ Straight wrist
- Material_____

Legs (check one)
- ☐ Ball jointed ☐ Bent limb ☐ Straight
- Material_____

Mark(s) on Body
- Where located_____
- Stamped, incised:_____
- Signed by ☐ Artist ☐ Manufacturer

Clothing (check one)
- ☐ Original to doll ☐ Contemporary with doll

Replacement clothing made by_____
_____

Outerwear
- Style_____
  _____
- Fabric_____
  _____
- Color_____
- Trim_____

Underwear
- Fabric_____
  _____
- Trim_____

Accessories_____
_____

References
References: (Book magazine article, internet)
- Source, author, page#_____
  _____
  _____

For a similar doll, see:_____
_____
_____

Ribbons & Awards:_____
_____
_____
_____